UNLOCKING THE PAST

Unlocking the Past

The impact of access to Barnardo's childcare records

GILL PUGH

Ashgate

Aldershot • Brookfield USA • Singapore • Sydney

Published by
Ashgate Publishing Ltd
Gower House
Croft Road
Aldershot
Hants GU11 3HR
England

Ashgate Publishing Company
Old Post Road
Brookfield
Vermont 05036
USA

Ashgate website: http://www.ashgate.com

British Library Cataloguing in Publication Data
Pugh, Gillian
    Unlocking the past : the impact of access to Barnardo's childcare records
    1. Barnardo's - Records and correspondence 2. Children - Institutional care - Great Britain - History - 20th century
    3. Adoptees - Family relationships
    I. Title
    362.7'3'0941

Library of Congress Catalog Card Number: 99-73394

ISBN 0 7546 1040 3

Printed and bound by Athenaeum Press, Ltd.,
Gateshead, Tyne & Wear.

Contents

Acknowledgements

This book is derived from a research thesis submitted for the degree of MA by Research at the School of Social Work, University of East Anglia, Norwich. Many thanks are due to the staff whose input on the MA course I valued highly, Dr Liz Trinder and Professor David Howe. I especially appreciate the contribution of my tutor Gill Schofield for her encouragement and constructive criticisms throughout the period of the study.

I would not have survived to complete the course and this book without the unfailing support and encouragement of my husband Steve, and the patience and good humour of my children Oliver and Laura when I ignored them and monopolised the computer for many long hours.

Whilst this study has been undertaken independently and in my own time, it has been enormously helpful to have the support and encouragement of my Manager, Collette Bradford, and colleagues in Barnardo's After Care, who have helped with advice, ideas, access to participants and typing of letters.

Most importantly, I am very grateful to all those who allowed me to interview them and use their experiences and reflections for this study. It was a pleasure and a privilege to meet them and I have learned much from them. Their contribution can only serve to increase awareness and understanding of the meaning of gaining access to their records, and to highlight the importance of providing quality services to meet their needs.

Gill Pugh

Introduction

... to shake the tree of life itself
And bring down fruit unheard of.
(Edwin Arlington Robinson)

In July 1995 the BBC broadcast a series of documentary films, *Barnardo's Children*, to commemorate 125 years of childcare by the charity. The films portrayed the work of Barnardo's since its founding in the 1860s up to the present day. Between 1866 and the early 1970s, Barnardo's was home to 350,000 children who spent all or part of their lives in its care in the UK, Canada and Australia. Some grew up in Barnardo's children's homes, some were fostered, others adopted, while some experienced a combination of care situations. Many of these children grew up unaware of their family backgrounds or reasons for being in care. The television documentaries illustrated both the early work of Barnardo's and the service it now offers to those formerly in its care who wish to discover their origins and make sense of their past.

Barnardo's received a massive response to the showing of these films. Their enquiry rates from adults seeking information about themselves rocketed from around 1,500 a year to an extra four thousand enquiries in the following weeks alone. Many of the enquirers had previously been unaware of the possibility of being able to see their records. For many the films stirred up long buried or forgotten memories and emotions, and aroused or revived a new hunger for information about themselves. Several new social work posts were created by Barnardo's to meet this huge and intense demand. Finding this an irresistibly fascinating area of work, I applied for, and was appointed to one of these posts.

In my new professional role, curiosity about the impact upon people who, in adulthood, sought and discovered highly emotionally-charged information about their origins, led me to the topic for this study. I sought to gain a better understanding of adults who approached Barnardo's and requested to see their personal files. I wanted to explore the impact upon those adults, who were generally in the middle or later years of their life, of reading information about their family background, the reasons for their admission to care and

1

what happened during their time in care. Did, for example, such information change the way in which people perceived themselves, or the way in which they were perceived by others around them? Did it have an effect upon people's self-esteem, or upon their relationships with significant others in their lives? Might the impact of the information be affected by factors such as the nature of the contents (whether the records contained difficult or painful information), or the manner in which the information was imparted? Would the person's previous life-experience affect the impact of receiving this information?

As a social worker working in the After Care Section of Barnardo's it was my job to prepare and share this information with such people, and to help them to try to make sense of the past. However the constraints of finite resources and a lengthy waiting list mean that long-term involvement or counselling of the people I saw was not possible, and the majority are seen by a social worker only once or twice. It is difficult to get a perspective of the effects of such an experience beyond the initial impact witnessed during the actual sharing of the records. Some choose to share their feelings and responses in subsequent contacts with the organisation through articles they write for the magazine for 'Old Boys and Girls' (as they are still commonly known) and through meetings at reunions of former residents. But there appeared to have been no formal or rigorous attempt to explore the impact of this experience. As I discovered upon undertaking the literature review for this study, research into adults who grew up in care generally is very sparse, and research into looking at care records appears to be virtually nonexistent, in contrast to the interest shown in access to birth records after adoption.

Through my social work practice I was aware that people requested access to their files for a variety of reasons, and with very varying expectations. The degree of prior knowledge of their family background or reasons for admission to care also varied widely from almost total ignorance of the past through the whole spectrum. I hoped that my study would begin to explain how these differences affected the process of seeing the records and what impact this produced.

The choice of topic for this study was influenced not only by personal and professional curiosity but by an understanding of its importance in a broader perspective. The developments within Barnardo's which have led to the opening up of its records for access by former residents need to be seen within the context of changes within society in general and changes in attitudes towards the family and childcare social work in particular. The 'child rescue' approach to child welfare of past years has been replaced by current legislation which emphasises partnership with, and support for, families. Parental contact with children in care, and increasingly post-adoption, is promoted more vigorously, and current policies recognise the importance of helping children to develop a strong sense of identity through knowledge and understanding of their origins. However Berridge (1997) notes the dearth of research into the impact of such developments, and whether the intentions behind the legislation have been fulfilled.

Post-adoption services for both adopted children and adults are expanding (see for example, Burnell and Briggs, 1997) to meet the demand for support with issues such as searching for information and tracing families. Despite some research interest following the implementation of access to birth records legislation for adopted people (for example, Day, 1979; Haimes and Timms, 1985; Walby and Symons, 1990; and more recently, Feast and Howe, 1997), many related areas, such as the long-term outcome of reunions with birth relatives, remain relatively unexplored (Feast and Howe, 1997).

Services for those formerly in care are also growing; the Children's Society for example has recently appointed its first worker to deal specifically with requests for information from its former care residents. Adults who grew up in care are increasingly feeling able to disclose their experiences of 'historical abuse', and a number of voluntary agencies are working together to develop policies and practice to meet their needs. Support for adults seeking access from local authorities to their care records appears however, from anecdotal and practice evidence, to be variable and often inadequate. As Social Services struggle to meet their statutory obligations, the needs of those seeking information from their records appear to receive low priority. Furthermore, records have often been destroyed or mislaid during reorganisations or moves over the years. However, the interest in, and demand for services to meet these needs continues to expand. It is important that provision is planned on a sound knowledge base if it is to lead to high quality practice. It is hoped that this study will contribute towards an understanding of the issues and implications of enabling people to make sense of their past.

The study is divided into three parts. Part 1 examines the literature around the topic of adults who grew up in care and seek information about their origins, and aims to place the subject in a wider context. It explores the historical context in which a culture of secrecy about origins has led to some adults growing up in ignorance of their past, and looks at the social and legal changes which have created a gradual transition away from severance of biological ties and towards greater openness and partnership with parents. The key themes from research into access to birth records by adoptees are examined, and their relevance to those seeking access to care records considered. In order to gain a better understanding of the impact upon the individuals who receive information about their past, Part 1 also explores what the literature tells us about the key issues of separation, loss, and how the experience of substitute care affects those who grow up apart from their birth families. Finally, Part 1 looks at the impact of gaining significant information about origins in the context of the literature on identity, and explores the relationship between an understanding of one's origins and the development of a sense of identity and self-esteem.

In Part 2, the methodology and findings of a qualitative study of 12 people who sought access to their Barnardo's records of their family background and time in care are presented. The impact upon them of receiving such information is explored, in the context of their experiences in childhood and beyond and their motivation for wanting to explore their past. The study explores their attitudes to their birth families, to Barnardo's, and to the impact upon themselves of living with ignorance and trying to make sense of the past.

The key themes which arose from the study, and their implications for current social work policy and practice, are discussed in Part 3.

PART 1
LITERATURE REVIEW

1   Secrecy and Openness in Child Welfare – A Historical Perspective

The history of substitute care for children reflects society's changing responses to the needs of children brought up apart from their parents. These responses have been determined by the interrelationship of social, cultural and political forces operating at any given time. The pendulum has at different times and in different contexts swung back and forth between belief in the severance of all links between birth parents and child (the 'fresh start' approach) and belief in the preservation of biological links and continuity. Severance of ties tends to be associated with a desire to suppress not only contact with, but knowledge of people and information from the past ('secrecy'). At the other end of the spectrum comes the promotion of ongoing contact and 'openness' between the separated child and his or her family of origin.

These polarities have been particularly well documented in the field of adoption, where current calls for more openness provide a major forum for debate in social work practice today. In trying to understand how and why these changes and trends have occurred, I aim to set in a historical perspective the situation of those adults who are now coming forward to Barnardo's and elsewhere seeking family background information and counselling.

I want to discover how the current situation has arisen whereby many adults have spent their childhoods in ignorance of the basic facts of their family background and reasons for coming into care. What was the reason behind the policy of secrecy or withholding of information, and why has this been overturned now?

Childhood and Society in the Nineteenth Century: Child-Rescue

My historical overview starts in the period when Dr Thomas Barnardo began his work, rescuing street children from poverty and homelessness in the East

End of London. Poverty, poor sanitation and child labour practices meant that infant mortality was high; in the 1870s one child in five died before their fifth birthday (Abstract of British Historical Statistics). Industrialisation and urbanisation were the backdrops to the Poor Law system and the legal separation of pauper children from their parents via the workhouse. It was, in Fox Harding's analysis, a period of 'state paternalism', when the survival of children was the main preoccupation and childcare was chiefly regarded as 'good economy and imperialism' (1991, p. 86).

Such concerns spawned the 'child-saving movement' to be found in the proliferation of philanthropic (and mainly religious) organisations which originated in the 1860s and 1870s. Rescuing children from the 'shame and degradation' of poverty, crime, overcrowding and disease was seen as a means of securing not only their physical survival but also their spiritual salvation. Emotional or psychological well-being was not a consideration. The biological family was not valued highly in the approaches to child protection, or 'rescuing'. Separation in these circumstances was deemed desirable and commendable.

Early Twentieth Century Development: Survival, Stigma and Secrecy

Childcare in the first half of the twentieth century was still predominantly concerned with the physical well-being of children. It was only in the 1920s that the infant mortality rate began to fall. Barnardo's records of this time show a marked emphasis on health issues – height and weight were regularly checked, and welfare visitors to foster homes recorded whether children were adequately nourished and looked 'sturdy'. Apart from checks that 'moral development' was being attended to (which in practice seemed to imply adherence to regular church attendance), there was a general lack of sensitivity to children's emotional needs. They were rarely consulted as to their own feelings or wishes, and their bonds with their families of origin were given low priority. Indeed, legislation such as the 1933 Children and Young Persons Act emphasised the importance attached to the removal of children from 'undesirable surroundings' into 'proper provision'. Complete severance of the blood tie was deemed desirable in these circumstances in order to achieve a 'fresh start'.

Extreme examples of this thinking were the child emigration schemes of this period whereby thousands of children were migrated by various charities from children's homes in Britain to new lives in distant parts of the Empire.

Once children had been separated from their parents, it became increasingly difficult for them to ever be restored. Even if the cause of the original separation was overcome, parents were treated with great suspicion if it was felt that they only wanted their children back because they had reached useful wage-earning ages. Secondly, many children were cared for at great distances from their parental homes (it was considered desirable to remove them from the corrupting influences of the city and into the fresh air of the countryside). Parental visiting then became an insuperable hurdle, often exacerbated by the rigid restrictions laid down by many agencies. This situation was not of course peculiar to this period. The hurdles faced by parents in maintaining contact with their children in care, and the effect this had in impeding rehabilitation, were highlighted again in the 1970s and 1980s (Rowe and Lambert, 1973; Millham et al., 1986).

Large numbers of both orphaned and illegitimate children following the 1914-18 war led to increasing demands for the establishment of legal adoption, and the passing of the 1926 Adoption Act. Traditionally, adoption has been the ultimate method of complete 'severance' of a child from its birth family. This was not however the intention of the Tomlin Committee who drew up the legislation in 1925. Their report frowned upon adoption agencies' attempts to 'fix a gulf between the child's past and future' (1925, p. 9). They attributed the agencies' desire for secrecy partly to the fear of interference by the natural parents, and partly to the belief that 'if the eyes be closed to the facts, the facts themselves will cease to exist so that it will be an advantage to an illegitimate child who has been adopted if in fact his origin cannot be traced' (p. 9). Ryburn (1995) noted that although the fears of interference were not borne out in practice, the wishes of the adoption agencies predominated. Secrecy gradually became enshrined in adoption legislation and practice and the rights of birth parents became eroded.

This trend in many ways influenced the thinking and practice in other areas of childcare in this period. A strong belief prevailed in the power of good parenting, and its ability to compensate for early deficiencies. It followed that the greater the separation of a child from its origins, the better the chance of 'success' in adoption or substitute care (Ryburn, 1995).

The preference for secrecy was reinforced by the surge of illegitimate births during and after the second world war, many born to married women while their husbands were away in the services. The stigma of illegitimacy and the wish for concealment in these circumstances must have been powerful, and Ryburn (1995) speculates on the possible influence of those affected who were 'well-connected' socially and politically.

The State of the Secrecy v. Openness Debate in the Second Half of the Twentieth Century

The examination of childcare philosophies over the last hundred years reveals how, for a number of reasons, children who were cared for away from their families were often completely severed from their roots and kept in ignorance of their origins. There were voices advocating alternative views, but these were drowned out by more powerful influences. The voice of the birth family, and especially the voice of the child, was rarely heard (Pugh, 1993).

The adults who are interviewed for this study, grew up in this period of 'secrecy'. Experience from practice at Barnardo's reveals that the younger enquirers, in their late 20s or early 30s, are usually more knowledgable about their past than their older counterparts. Their desire for information is often more to do with trying to make sense of the past than with filling in large gaps in their history. So how has this change come about, and where in the spectrum does today's childcare practice lie?

Economic growth and prosperity were a feature of the post-war period for many. Infant mortality rates fell by 65 per cent between 1963 and 1991 (OPCS, 1992). The creation of the welfare state and the passing of the 1948 Children Act heralded an unprecedented expansion in the social services, and the psychological needs of children began to receive increased attention. There was a marked shift away from institutional care towards foster care and the substitute family life it was supposed to provide (Parker, 1990).

A strong desire developed to undertake preventative work and assist families before they broke down. Fox Harding describes the 1960s as the peak time for the 'defence of the family and parental rights' (1991). Bowlby's theories on maternal deprivation, advocating the importance of a constant mother attachment free from interruption (1951), were already influential in childcare training. Several significant research studies served to reinforce the trend towards preventative work by highlighting the emotional damage to children of high breakdown rates in fostering (Trasler, 1960; Parker, 1966; George, 1970).

Rowe and Lambert's study (1973) exposed the fact that many children were 'drifting' in care, with little planning for either restoration or permanency. A major barrier to rehabilitation home was seen to be the erosion of contact between children in care and their families. Increasingly, efforts and resources were devoted to trying to keep children in care in touch with their parents, as a means of achieving earlier restoration. However, mounting concern for continuity and stability for those children for whom restoration was not seen to be viable led to the sometimes aggressive pursuit of 'permanence' policies. Here was the redefinition of the 'fresh start' approach.

Childcare research generally increased around this time, and exercised a significant influence upon social work and political agendas. However, much research of the 1970s and 1980s was conflicting in its messages about 'fresh starts' or preservation of ties. Goldstein, Freud and Solnit (1973 and 1979) for example advocated (based on clinical experience) severing past links in order that children could make secure attachments to their new substitute families. Considerable importance was attached to such views by social work agencies at the time. On the other hand, studies such as Triseliotis (1973) and McWhinnie (1967) highlighted the devastating effects of secrecy in adoption on identity and psychological well-being and emphasised the need for knowledge about one's origins.

Policies and practice both reflect and influence social change. Over the last few decades, the stigma attached to illegitimacy and single parenthood has gradually relaxed, though not disappeared. The growing attention paid (belatedly) to the needs of black children and families has brought new cultural awareness and perceptions about the capacity of the family for 'inclusive' relationships (Holman, 1980). There has been a general demand for greater openness from government and bureaucracies, and for the right of access to all kinds of records kept on us by organisations. A rise in consumerism has fostered the growth of self-help groups to articulate the needs of hitherto neglected causes. In the childcare field this has included NORCAP (National Organisation for the Counselling of Adoptees and Parents) which supports adoptees searching for information, PPIAS (Parent to Parent Information on Adoption Services) and NAYPIC, the National Association for Young People in Care (Parker, 1990; Pugh, 1993).

The 'Children's Rights' movement has been especially influential in the trend towards greater openness in childcare. It advocates the importance of hearing the child's own views and wishes, instead of accepting adults' rights to determine what is best for children. Similar developments have occurred in many parts of the world, and were marked by the 1989 UN Convention on the Rights of the Child. This stated explicitly the right of children to information about themselves, and the right to have a say in decisions affecting their lives. It also highlighted the importance of preserving children's identity (Article 8). The 1989 Children Act declared that the child's welfare should be the 'paramount' consideration. The presumption is – once more – that children are usually best kept in their own families, and 'accommodation' is provided (whether in foster- or residential care) as a service to support the child in his or her biological family. 'Partnership' between the family and the state is emphasised.

Access to Personal Records: The Legal Framework

There are currently two main areas of legislation concerning adults who are seeking their birth records, or records relating to their time in care. In England and Wales adopted people over the age of 18 were given the right of access to their original birth records in section 26 of the 1975 Children Act. This clause came into effect in November 1976. These provisions were also brought into section 51 of the Adoption Act 1976 which was fully implemented on 1 January 1988. This legislation entitles adoptees over 18 to information which will enable them to obtain a copy of their original birth certificate. Anyone adopted before 12 November 1975 must attend a counselling interview to receive their information.

Counselling is intended to ensure that adoptees are fully aware of the possible implications for themselves and others of tracing their birth parent or family, although in practice the role of the counsellor may encompass many aspects. It provides an opportunity for adoptees to explore their feelings about their own adoption and their expectations of their birth family, as well as helping them to make sense of their information.

Similar provisions for adoptees were introduced in Northern Ireland in 1987 (Adoption [Northern Ireland] Order 1987). Adoptees in Scotland have had a right of access to their birth records since 1930. This is now enshrined in the Adoption [Scotland] Act, 1978, section 45, and is applicable to any adopted person over 17 years old. Counselling is available but not compulsory.

The provisions of the 1975 Children Act (section 26) and related legislation represented such a dramatic breaking with the tradition of secrecy in adoption that it gave rise to a profusion of studies in the years following its implementation. It was always recognised that a great deal could be learned from this new situation not just about adoption, but also about the significance to the individual of gaining information about his or her origins. These research studies are examined in chapter 2.

Outside of the adoption field, the principle legislation governing those who seek access to information about their past which is held in official records is the Access to Personal Files Act 1987 and the associated Access to Personal Files (Social Services) Regulations 1989.

This legislation enables an individual to know what is recorded about him in the manually maintained records held by a local authority for the performance of its 'social services functions' (as defined in the Local Authority Social Services Act 1970). This includes material held in files, day books and that used in care proceedings. However, unlike the data protection legislation, this legislation does not apply to the records of voluntary organisations, even if they are acting as agents of a local authority.

The Department of Health Guidance Notes (LAC[89]2) set out restrictions on access to third party information and, in 'exceptional circumstances', where it is considered that access to personal information might result in 'serious harm' to the physical or mental health or emotional condition of the individual or some other person. However in general it refers positively to the benefits for the individual of making available as much information as possible, to facilitate 'a greater clarity and understanding of an individual's background'.

Voluntary childcare agencies such as Barnardo's or the Children's Society are not bound by this legislation and are free to be as restrictive or progressive over access to their records as they choose. In general, practice seems to be guided by the legislation applicable to local authorities. In most cases, agencies who allow access to records have also recognised the importance of 'counselling' for those seeking access to their birth or family background records, and this is usually a mandatory prerequisite of obtaining access.

Practice has also been significantly influenced by the principles of the European Convention on Human Rights, which was ratified by the UK in 1969, and subsequent rulings of the European Court. One case in particular has been influential – that of Gaskin v. UK (12 EHRR 36; 7 July 1989). Mr Gaskin had spent most of his life in the care of Liverpool City Council, and sought access to his social services records. His request was refused in part on the ground that some of the information had originally been given in confidence and certain of the informants did not consent to their material being disclosed. The Court concluded that the local authority had a legitimate claim, but so too did Gaskin, because the information was necessary in order to understand his childhood and identity The Court found that a balancing of the conflicting interests was required and ruled that there had been a violation of Article 8 of the Convention, which safeguards the right to respect for one's private and family life (1989).

The Gaskin judgement provides the individual with protection against interference by public authority, but allows considerable discretion in the law which a state adopts. It implies that the rights of those cared for by private or charitable organisations need to be protected as if they had been cared for by a public authority.

In conclusion, it is however important to note that a legal right of access to information is only of value if there is public awareness of that right. Whilst, with the help of the media, awareness is growing, there is an on-going need to ensure that those who most need this information are made aware of what is available and how to obtain access to it.

Conclusion

Some would claim that those adults now seeking to plug the information gaps about themselves and their origins are a dying generation – the end of an era in which ignorance of the past was promoted in the name of (at best) protecting the child's best interests. Historical, social, cultural and political forces have combined to produce fundamental changes in the way society deals with children and the family. Research has played its part in both highlighting those changes and influencing thinking and policy-making into new directions.

It would however be an oversimplification to suggest that the general trend away from secrecy and towards greater openness can be traced along a straightforward continuum. Whilst the current state of childcare thinking and practice may be located somewhere near the 'openness' extremity when viewed across time, it is argued by some that there is still plenty of room for further movement in that direction. Meanwhile an understanding of the forces which shaped their history can only help to improve services for those who still need support to make sense of their past.

2 Searching for Origins and Access to Birth Records

The literature which addresses the impact upon adults who receive family background information later in life is dominated by a focus on adoption. Adoption in general, and access to birth records by adoptees in particular, have received considerable attention in the literature, in contrast to the paucity of studies of the non-adopted care population. The reasons for this may be speculated on. There are difficulties in defining, and therefore in making comparisons with or drawing conclusions from such an amorphous and varied group as the 'care population'. (I use this term to include those who have spent all or a substantial part of their childhoods in substitute care, whether residential or foster-care, in the state or voluntary sectors.) Furthermore this group, in contrast to adoptees, lacks a comparable legislative framework to cover their rights of access to birth records. Consequently the service they receive is inconsistent, and has not been publicised in the same way as recent adoption legislation. However, it seems likely that the literature concerning adoptees' access to their birth records may have considerable relevance to the searches made by the subjects of this study, so this chapter examines and analyses the major themes of the research in this area.

Key Themes from the Research

(a)   Motivation for the Search

> Two of the most common motives reported in the *empirical* literature include the desire for background information and wish to make contact with a birth relative (Feast and Howe, 1997, p. 8).

Triseliotis (1973) interviewed 70 Scottish adoptees who had sought their birth records and found that they fell into two distinct groups: those who wanted to find a birth parent, and those who simply wanted to obtain background genealogical information. He found the former group to be more strongly motivated, and described a 'great sense of urgency' about their enquiries (p. 108). However from a comparison of the numbers of adoptees who sought access to their records with the overall population of adoptees, he concluded that *any* searching activity was a minority response. Seeking to understand the distinguishing features of this minority he looked at connections between the quality of the adoptive experience and the desire to search. From this, Triseliotis concluded that:

> ... the majority of adoptees searching into their genealogical background and especially most, but not all, of those trying to find their birth parents were unhappy and lonely people and a considerable number had had psychiatric help. They generally hoped that the search would lead to new nurturing relationships or at least to the development of a more secure personality (p. 160).

The poorer the adoptive experience, the stronger was felt to be the desire to search and trace. The motivation of adoptees was not the product of natural curiosity, but sprang from a 'deeply felt psychological need' (p. 154).

These findings were confirmed to some extent by Day (1979). In this study of 500 adoptees counselled by the General Register Office, those with unhappy adoptive experiences were found to be more likely to want to trace a parent than those with happy ones. The prime motivation for the search expressed by 53 per cent of all applicants was the need to establish or complete a sense of 'true self-identity'. However, these findings are not supported by most subsequent studies. Haimes and Timms (1985) conclude that:

> The wish to correct present relationships by tracing natural parents is only one feature in the process, and one which unduly emphasises the psycho-pathological image of the adopted person (p. 50).

Haimes and Timms (1985) interviewed 45 adoptees who had received Section 26 counselling. They looked not just at the personal significance for adoptees of access to birth records, but also at the broader issues of the identity of adoptees within society which were raised. In contrast to Triseliotis (1973), they argued that the desire to trace is more about adoptees 'seeking to place themselves socially', and also 'seeking to correct their marginal status' (p. 50) which has arisen, they argue, from adoptees' ignorance of their heritage. Walby and Symons (1990) also found that their respondents did not fit the pattern identified by Triseliotis. They interviewed 33 adoptees from one area in Wales who had been referred by the General Register Office for counselling between 1976 and 1978. While they acknowledged the likelihood that those with bad adoptive experiences, or very little information, will be highly motivated to search, they found no definitive reason why some adoptees seek information and others do not. The main motivation identified by their respondents was 'the quest for self-identity through biographical information and meeting blood relatives' (p. 69). Brodzinsky (1987) concluded that the desire to search is normal, and saw it as an extra developmental task which adoptees need to complete as part of their psychosocial adjustment.

A number of common 'triggers' were noted by several researchers (e.g. Triseliotis, 1973; Walby, 1982; Lindsay and McGarry, 1984) when they questioned why respondents embarked on their search for information at a particular time. These were:

- marriage or divorce;
- birth of a baby;
- need for family medical histories; and
- death of adoptive parents.

These 'life-cycle' triggers may go some way to explaining the pattern of age and sex characteristics of adoptees who seek access to their birth records. A fairly consistent trend can be seen in the research studies for the majority of applicants for access to be female, with a large percentage being in the 20–35 age group (Feast and Howe, 1997). A significant trigger identified for Walby and Symons's 1990 sample (possibly applicable in some other studies too) was the publicity surrounding the change in adoption law.

Hodgkins (1991) sums up the experience of specialist self-help agencies such as NORCAP (National Organisation for the Counselling of Adoptees and Parents) and the Post-Adoption Centre, regarding the motivation of applicants for access to birth records. The results of their postal survey of adopted adults who had traced their birth families following contact with NORCAP indicates that:

- applicants for birth records counselling express various opinions about adoption; and
- the need to know about origins relates to an individual's concept of self-identity rather than to any external pressures (Hodgkins, 1991, p. 14).

Only a few, generally more recent studies from the post-adoption field (e.g. Feast, 1992; Sawbridge, 1990) acknowledge that their research is based on a largely white user perspective. This may reflect the fact that until the 1970s and 1980s black children were often not placed for adoption, but remained in the care system. Sawbridge (1988) reports that, at the time of writing, all the black adopted people seen by the Post-Adoption Centre had been transracially adopted. Meanwhile it needs to be acknowledged that the black perspective in the majority of studies of access to birth records has been largely omitted by researchers.

(b)   Aims and Expectations of Those who Search

The various studies agree that about half of those seeking access are only after additional information to 'complete themselves' and are not seeking meetings or reunions with original parents (Triseliotis, 1984, p. 42).

The majority wanted to find out about *both* birth parents and possible siblings. Some particularly wanted medical details, and for others physical details assumed great importance 'as being necessary to develop a self body-image and also to attach a distinctiveness to their children' (Triseliotis, 1973). One adoptee is quoted as commenting, 'If I had some description of my birth parents, it might help me recognise myself' (p. 152). The other crucial question to which answers were sought was whether or not the adoptees' birth parents had loved them, and why they had given them up:

> [They] wanted to see their original parents as loving and caring, but the fact of their surrender was preventing them from completing this picture ... The confirmation of a 'good' and 'caring' parental figure would help to raise their own self-esteem as 'caring' and 'good' people (Triseliotis, 1973, p. 110).

Haimes and Timms (1985) made the point that some adoptees' expectations of the 'Section 26' counselling process had been influenced by media coverage of the new provision, which 'tended to emphasise the more sensational aspects, particularly that of actual reunions between adoptees and natural parents' (p. 51). In their sample of 45 adoptees, 23 wanted to trace a birth relative. This was almost always their mother, though sometimes apparently only for reasons of expediency, such as the anticipated difficulties of tracing other relatives. Haimes and Timms noted the 'lack of an available script' to explain the unusual quest of wanting to know who your parents are, without wishing to appear in any way abnormal or obsessed.

A different factor found by Walby and Symons (1990) to influence adoptees' objectives in their search for information was 'the practical help and advice available and the explicit and implicit sanctions applied by those around them' (p. 69). The need for secrecy from adoptive parents in particular compounded the hurdles for some of their respondents, and females particularly were found to feel guilty about what they perceived as 'a self-indulgent activity'.

Walby and Symons established a voluntary follow-up discussion group of adoptees who had participated in their research. This revealed that many individuals had developed their search for information much further since the time of the study. Walby and Symons thus commented upon the dangers of reaching over-hasty conclusions about the motivation and objectives of searchers, and surmised that respondents:

> ... at the point of counselling (and therefore of much research on the subject) ... are not only likely to be highly defensive but may also be only at the start of a long process (1990, p. 77).

Hodgkins (1991) warns counsellors that applicants for counselling 'may not be completely frank about their aims and intentions' (p. 24); they may feel they have to pass a 'test of suitability' in order to obtain their information, and thus be careful about their responses. Shekleton (1990) notes that such anxieties are often especially acute amongst transracially adopted adults, who may fear more than others that expressing their desire for information may be interpreted as evidence of instability.

(c)   Adoption Experiences of Searchers

Triseliotis (1973) found that almost half the adoptees in his study regarded their adoptive home relationships as unsatisfactory, and their adoption as a failure or mainly a failure. Over half of these had received psychiatric help (p. 58). Neither the social class nor the age of the adoptive parents appeared to be significant factors. The respondents described a failure to develop a sense of attachment and belonging. McWhinnie (1967) similarly found that adoptees who decided to search appeared to report less satisfactory adoptions, while Aumend and Barrett (1984) found that 'non-searchers expressed more positive attitudes about the effect of adoption on their feelings about themselves than did searchers'.

The influence of this work led many to believe that the desire to search (and especially, to trace) was generally associated with an unhappy experience of adoption. This however is not supported by many subsequent studies.

Haimes and Timms (1985) comment on the difficulty of actually assessing the quality of their respondents' adoptive experiences given 'their acknowledged complicity in the closed nature of their adoptive family life' (p. 67). However they judge that 'few of them seem to have had unhappy adoptions', adding that concern to preserve their relationship with their adoptive parents was a common feature which many had expressed anxiety about during the search. Similar findings emerged from both Hodgkins' study (1987) and a Barnardo's study of reunions between adoptees and their birth families (Parish and Cotton, 1989). Adoptees often waited until the death of their adoptive parents before embarking on their search through feelings of 'guilt' about disloyalty or fear of upsetting them. None of the studies produced consistent evidence to support the notion that searching is symptomatic of unsatisfactory experiences in the adoptive family.

Many in Walby and Symons' 1990 study expressed anger about being denied information to which they felt entitled, and feelings of stigmatisation about their adoptive state. Walby and Symons found that the critical factor in how respondents felt about their adoptive experiences, and consequently about themselves, was:

> ... the ability of the adoptive parents to recognise and share in the feelings of the adopted child about adoption, and particularly their appreciation of the child's need to explore the question, who am I? (1990, p. 68).

(d)   Outcome of the Search

It is difficult, and perhaps dangerous, to attempt to generalise from the wide variety of experiences and perceptions described by adoptees following their search for information. However, certain issues or themes do tend to recur throughout the literature. Perhaps the most important finding common to most studies (recent and less recent) is summed up by Parish and Cotton (1989) as, 'Good outcomes are not necessarily happy outcomes'. Their study looked specifically at adoptees whose search had led on to reunions with birth relatives. Some reunions, whilst often initially exciting and satisfying, had proved stressful and not long-lasting. But even in the latter instances, most respondents felt that they had satisfied a need to know about their origins, and felt more fulfilled by it, for example:

> I don't regret doing the tracing even though it didn't work out. I'm certainly easier to live with as I've satisfied my need to know about my past (1989, p. 14).

Triseliotis (1973) reported that eight out of ten of his adoptees were 'glad' about what information they obtained including most of those whose information was generally 'unpalatable' (p. 125). Comments included: 'I feel more at peace with myself', or, 'it helped me bridge the gap', or 'I feel less restless'.

Reactions of searchers to revelations were understandably linked with their previous expectations, many of which seemed to have a considerable element of wishful fantasy about them. Consequently many had experienced disappointments, describing themselves after the search as 'shattered', 'depressed' or 'confused'. Triseliotis points out however that this did not necessarily mean they regretted their search, but referred rather to the difficulties of integrating new realities with past fantasies (p. 130).

Haimes and Timms (1985) distinguished between those of their respondents who felt able to assimilate their new knowledge into their present lives, and conversely those who seemed to need to construct an *alternative* life-history – a pre- and post-adoption image of themselves. Either way, they also made comments such as: 'it gives you a little bit more of an identity', and 'a feeling of completion, of certainty' (p. 71).

The sensitivity of most respondents to the issue of illegitimacy seems to refute the notion of some that this is no longer a source of stigma. Triseliotis (1973) found – even in the 1970s – that the confirmation of illegitimacy, even when previously known or suspected, often aroused feelings of shame and inferiority, and anxiety about perceived community attitudes, for example,

> ... it is shattering to find out. You are suddenly left bare and you think, 'I am only a bastard' ... how do you explain that to your children? (1973, p. 126).

Confirmation of illegitimacy seemed to reinforce an already poor self-image in adoptees. Those (few) adoptees who found that they were *not* illegitimate, though relieved on one score, often felt less able to understand their rejection. They felt generally less sympathetic to their parents' actions.

The discovery of a surname of possible foreign origin was another source of confusion and threat to cultural identity highlighted by Triseliotis (1973). The important issues of ethnic and racial identity for those seeking information about their roots are discussed further in chapter 4.

In all the studies, the amount and nature of information to which respondents managed to gain access from their records varied enormously. Many were disappointed with the paucity of the information available.

(e)   Personal and Social Identity

These themes recurred prominently throughout the literature on adults who sought information about their origins. The relevance of identity to the subject of this study appears to be so central that it is addressed separately in chapter 4, when the key research findings from access to records studies are examined in the context of clinical and psychological literature about identity.

Adults who Grow up in Care and Search for Their Origins

Some researchers in the adoption field have made reference to the quest for roots amongst those who have not been adopted. Triseliotis (1984) claims that recent adoption studies have:

> ... yielded insights into the subject of identity which are relevant to the
> development of self – not only among adoptees but in all children, particularly
> those growing up in situations where one or both carers are not the birth parents
> (1984, p. 41).

He examines the evidence from both adoption research, and also his own (substantial) studies in the fields of residential and foster-care (e.g. Triseliotis, 1980; Triseliotis and Russell, 1984). From these he concludes that:

> There is a psychosocial need in all people, manifest principally among those
> who grow up away from their original families, to know about their background,
> their genealogy and their personal history if they are to grow up feeling complete
> and whole (1984, p. 38).

Triseliotis has apparently moved on from the suggestion drawn from his 1973 study that the desire to search indicated a certain degree of psychopathology. He adds, however, that research suggests that the universal 'need to know' is 'intensified where secrecy and evasiveness predominate, and where relationships are not satisfactory' (1984, p. 40).

Lindsay and McGarry's study of users of the telephone counselling service set up by Barnardo's in Scotland (1984) included a few non-adopted adults who had grown up in care. Although the numbers were small (12 in all), the characteristics and needs of this group were found to be distinctively different in many ways from the adopted callers. Many spoke of traumatic background histories, of frequent moves and physical and sexual abuse. Their main reasons for calling tended to be a wish to unravel their background a little, make sense of hazy memories and sort out 'who was who' of the many adults who were involved with them during their childhood. A desire to search for birth parents often seemed less important when 'so many significant people have also "got lost" since the first parental link was broken' (1984, p. 43).

The authors found that the counselling services needed by such clients had to be especially sensitive due to the likelihood that their background information would be traumatic and upsetting, and that these callers needed more time to explore their feelings fully with someone.

Conclusion

Adoption research into access to birth records under Section 51 of the 1975 Children Act is likely to shed considerable light on issues related to adults who have not been adopted but who, having grown up apart from their families of birth, seek information about their origins. The themes described in the research tend to be reflected in a number of published autobiographical accounts of adoptees who have undergone searches for birth relatives, such as Begley (1988) or Copeman (1989). Such individuals give detailed accounts not just of the process of their searches, but also of the motivation behind their decisions to search, their hopes and fears, and the emotions engendered throughout the experience. A paucity of research into adults who grew up in care makes it difficult to test the key themes of the adoption literature against the experiences of the non-adopted group. However such available evidence as there is suggests that there may be many similarities in the characteristics and experiences of the two groups, but also significant factors which set them apart.

In order to seek a better understanding of the differences between those who grew up in care and those who were adopted, the following chapter examines the significance of separation, loss and discontinuity in their early lives, and the ways in which these experiences may shape people's attitudes towards finding out about their origins.

3   Separation, Loss and the Experience of Substitute Care

Looking at the historical context in which people who grew up in care seek information about their origins later in life highlighted the culture of secrecy which predominated in the period during which the subjects of this study spent their early lives. This chapter examines the significance of other factors which affected the developmental pathways and patterns which shaped people's lives. Evidence from the literature indicates that the impact of gaining information about one's roots as an adult can only be fully understood in the context of the influences upon development throughout the lifespan. The central themes which recur in the literature concerning those who grow up apart from their birth families are separation and loss. These are closely linked to the concept of attachment. These themes are therefore examined in an attempt to lend more meaning to the implications of both ignorance of one's origins and later, of overcoming that ignorance.

Child development theory emphasises the importance of continuity during the child's earliest years for the achievement of trust, security and attachment. It is therefore implicit that early separation from or loss of a parent (or other primary attachment figure) will have a major impact on a child's emotional and social development, and possibly on his cognitive and physical development as well (Bowlby, 1973; Robertson and Robertson, 1977; Fahlberg, 1981). However, the lives of those who grow up in care are characterised by the experience of discontinuity, separation and loss.

The experience of loss and grieving is well documented in social work and psychology literature (for example, Bowlby, 1969; Kubler-Ross, 1972; Fahlberg, 1981). Both children and adults experience a range of emotions during the stages of mourning. Their response will be determined by a number of key factors. The first of these is their experience of attachment prior to separation. Howe's research on adoption (1996, 1997) shows a distinctive pattern of developmental pathways which could be traced from children's pre-placement experiences through to their behaviour patterns as adults. The age of the child at separation is significant, for various reasons. Rutter (1981)

24

for example believes that 'children below the age of six or seven months are relatively immune because they have not yet developed selective attachments and therefore are not able to experience separation and anxiety' (p. 337). Howe's outcome studies (1997) of children placed for adoption after the age of six months reveal a significantly higher risk of problem behaviours than for those placed earlier, and particularly so where there was abuse, rejection or neglect prior to placement.

Cultural reactions to separation and loss are likely to influence a child's ability to resolve his or her feelings. Both Jewett (1984) and Lifton (1988) argue that a major problem for separated children in Western cultures is the denial of mourning rituals:

> There is no ritual ceremony, like lighting candles or sitting shivah, to mourn parents who are as if dead, while never having been as if legitimately alive (Lifton, 1988, p. 41).

Black children's difficulties with loss may be exacerbated by the loss of cultural reference points (Cheetham, 1972) or identity confusion in transracial placements (e.g. Small, 1986).

Aldgate (1988) identifies other important factors which may influence a child's (or adult's) response to separation and loss as 'gender, temperament, cognitive appraisal and set, and social circumstances before and after separation' (p. 39). 'Cognitive set' is defined by Aldgate as 'a sense of self-esteem which makes successful coping more likely' (p. 41). She refers to Rutter's findings (1985) that those most likely to develop a positive cognitive set are those who, within the context of their own culture and community, have been exposed to 'secure, stable affectional relationships, and experiences of success and achievement'.

This relates to the factors discussed elsewhere in this study regarding the nature of the care experience undergone by the child after separation from his or her family of origin (for example, whether he or she was fostered or brought up in a residential institution, the quality of that care, and the number of moves experienced). It is also a pertinent reminder of the importance of understanding cultural, ethnic and racial differences.

The final key factor likely to influence an individual's reaction to separation, and to help determine the long-term outcome, is the support which is received to cope with that loss. Aldgate (1988), drawing on a variety of sources, lists the circumstances most likely to promote children's recovery. These are, firstly, the stability and quality of relationships with adults, and secondly, the psychological and physical health of parents (where children are reunited). The most adverse reactions are likely, she says, if the separated child subsequently experiences multiple carers and little stability. This is amply confirmed by other research (e.g. Rowe and Lambert, 1973).

Fahlberg (1981) describes the result of insufficient help given to children in resolving loss issues as the child becoming psychologically 'stuck' at the age of the loss of their primary attachment object. She says:

> Although the effects of parent loss can never be totally obliterated, the negative impact can be minimised if, during the grieving process, the child lives in an environment which is supportive of re-establishing psychological equilibrium.

Brodzinsky (1990) outlines a model of adaptive grieving which he applies to the loss of the mother who surrenders an infant for adoption. It would seem however equally applicable to the child experiencing the loss of a parent. His five criteria for successful resolution of loss are:

i)   safety – through a supportive network of family and friends;
ii) freedom to express feelings and to behave differently (often culturally determined);
iii) proximity, empathy and warmth (the need to be understood);
iv) rituals for passing. Just as relinquishing an infant for adoption is not recognised by society with any ritual or farewell, neither generally is the entry of a child into the care system and accompanying loss of family by separation (on the contrary, stigma and secrecy are the more probable response); and
v)   opportunity for reorganisation – trying to redefine one's identity in a world without the lost one. Opportunities for the separated child are dependent upon the availability of effective support from adults.

Today, the concepts of separation and loss are very familiar in the vocabulary of social work, but effective strategies for helping children deal with loss have been slower to develop. Those adults who grew up in an era where openness about origins was not the norm are also those who suffered from a lack of attention paid to the importance and impact of their losses. Denied the information about their heritage which they required to achieve a sense of identity and self-esteem, then faced with a lack of recognition or support for their need to grieve their loss, the negative psychological impact upon such individuals must surely be considerable.

The Impact of Substitute Care

This section examines further evidence from the literature about important influences during people's lives which may increase our understanding of the significance of gaining information about origins later in life. Access to birth records research suggests that there may be a link between people's motivation to search for information or to trace relatives and the quality of the care they received in childhood (chapter 2). This section explores whether there is evidence to indicate that a particular type of substitute care received (e.g. residential, foster-care or adoption) may have made a difference to people's need to know about their backgrounds, perhaps because of the way in which it met, or failed to meet, the child's needs.

Residential care and especially foster care are very much the 'poor relations' when it comes to research compared with adoption (Berridge, 1997). The need has only relatively recently been recognised to develop measures to assess outcomes of different social work interventions with children looked after away from home (Department of Health, 1995; Ward, 1995). The 'Looking after Children' project gives the potential for significant future improvements in awareness of the needs of children looked after away from home and of how these may be met.

Although there has been a growing body of research undertaken particularly since the 1970s into the impact of different types of substitute care, it must be remembered that the adults who are the subjects of my study grew up in care in the 1920s–60s. Whilst more recent research may cast light on many of the questions posed about their experiences, it needs to be considered in the context of the childcare theories and ideologies which flourished in earlier times. The large, all-encompassing residential institutions which Barnardo's established in the early part of the century for example all closed about 30 years ago. Even the use of smaller residential settings has declined in favour of increased family care in both the state and voluntary sectors. More importantly there has been increasing questioning of earlier assumptions about the wisdom of separating deprived children from their families and denying them contact (Parker, 1990).

Research over a long period consistently shows that the experience of multiple moves in care is unfortunately all too common (Parker, 1966; Berridge and Cleaver, 1987; Rowe, Hundleby and Garnett, 1989), and is significant in influencing impact and outcomes:

> The youngster who has spent the major part of his life in care is often uncertain
> about why he came into care, why changes in placement were made, why other
> children moved on and why staff left; he may not know the names of various
> people who have looked after him, let alone their current whereabouts; the same
> is true regarding the children who shared his life for certain periods; nor does
> he know what the future is likely to hold since long-term plans are rarely made
> (Page and Clark, 1977, p. 134, in Pringle, 1980).

There are few research studies comparing the long-term adjustment of
children and adults who have experienced different types of care. There are
however two significant recent British studies, by Triseliotis and Russell (1984)
and Hill, Lambert and Triseliotis (1989). The evidence from both these pieces
of research was analysed by Triseliotis and Hill (1990). They identified three
important factors which appeared to contribute to the development of personal
and social identity, including a sense of security. These were:

- quality of care experienced;
- knowledge about origins and past; and
- being part of the wider community with no stigma attached (p. 120).

Triseliotis and Hill (1990) found a continuum of experiences between those
who had experienced different types of care. Adoptees, unsurprisingly, seemed
to have experienced the most consistent and intimate care and closest
attachments to their caregivers. In contrast the residential group felt a lack of
closeness, individual attention and continuity of care. They attributed these to
frequent staff changes, lack of privacy, and the impersonality and stigma
attached to institutional life. The residential care group was reported to have
expressed least confidence in 'their ability to form relationships, cope with
life's demands and carry out parenting roles' (p. 112). Those who had
experienced mainly foster care fell somewhere between the other two groups.
    The main conclusion of Triseliotis and Hill is that:

> Those growing up adopted, even if placed when older, appear in adulthood to
> have a stronger sense of self and to function more adequately at the personal,
> social and economic level compared with those who were formerly fostered,
> and particularly, those who grew up for a large part of their lives in institutions.
> Furthermore, adoption has a greater potential for reversing earlier adverse
> experiences than foster and residential care (p. 107).

These findings are supported by Rutter, Quinton and Liddle (1983). They found that children from residential care backgrounds encountered more social problems as adults and were more likely to become poor parents. On the other hand, Bullock (1993) found that residential care confers educational benefits, and could offer children stability in an otherwise disrupted life. Berridge and Brodie (1996) pointed out a number of common deficiencies which affected both services, particularly, caring for children from ethnic minority groups, and adequate concern for health and educational needs. They note that several studies of young people's views about care have been largely positive (Page and Clarke, 1977; Kahan, 1979; and more recently, Triseliotis et al., 1995). However, despite the changes in childcare policy and practice since the period in which the subjects of this study grew up, recent 'consumer' research (e.g. Fletcher, 1993) still highlights a call for 'greater efforts to be made to keep families together and to maintain contact once received into care' (Freeman et al., 1996).

Despite the paucity of research evidence and the methodological difficulties in assessing outcomes studies, there are nevertheless indications that the quality and nature of substitute care received may significantly influence the developmental pathways into and throughout adult life. An awareness of these influences, combined with people's responses to their exceptional experiences of separation and loss, help to make sense of the need for information about their origins in adulthood. When severance and discontinuity has been a prominent feature in people's lives, the importance of finding one's roots assumes a much greater significance.

4   Heritage, Identity and Self-esteem

> [The] 'growing up' tasks of achieving a mature independence and a clear sense of identity, and being able to give and receive love ... are inextricably linked with knowledge and feelings about heritage and about how other people see us and behave towards us (Walby and Symons, 1990, p. 39).

The concepts of identity and self-esteem run powerfully throughout the literature on those who grow up in care or are adopted and seek information about their origins. This chapter draws on the literature and research evidence to examine further the 'inextricable links' between the achievement of a sense of identity and a knowledge of origins, or heritage, for the individual throughout their lifespan. It seeks to shed light on the significance of the blood tie, and the impact upon those for whom this tie is broken in early childhood. Theories are examined about how identity is formed, and about the various aspects of personal, social and cultural identity. Evidence is sought of the impact of a lack of knowledge of heritage upon identity and self-esteem.

What is Identity?

It is difficult to find an all-encompassing definition of identity. Triseliotis commented:

> ... it is easier perhaps to recognise the person who lacks this quality and feels the impoverishment of human ties, the inability to love and to relate ... (1973, p. 79).

One can distinguish several aspects of 'identity'. There is the sense of personal identity – 'an internal, self-constructed dynamic organisation of drives, abilities and individual history' (Marcia, 1980). However identity is concerned not simply with the internal workings of the mind, but with 'a compound of other multiple family, personal and socio-cultural influences'

(Triseliotis, 1973, p. 80). For the developing child this involves the:

> ... gradual identification and assimilation of confirmatory experiences about his own parents, his ancestors, his people, his country and its history (Triseliotis, 1973, p. 80).

Triseliotis stresses the need for adopted children 'to have information about their biological and sociological background to help them complete their self-image' (p. 81) and says that the strength and quality of the individual's identity determines their ability to cope with life situations and relationships.

Social identity may emerge from the reflected images of myths and legends, as well as through legal and social structures. It is a means of distinguishing one group of people with common characteristics from another. Haimes and Timms (1985, p. 77) suggest that:

> The enquiries which adoptees make about their past, including those under section 26, signify an acknowledgement of their differences and further, present an attempt to account for it.

For those who were not only reared apart from their birth parents, but also brought up by carers of a different cultural or racial background, there are additional challenges to face in the formation of a clear sense of personal and social identity. Each of these 'differences' will be examined more carefully in order to seek a greater understanding of identity issues for this group of people, and to try to make sense of how acquiring knowledge about their origins and roots is likely to impact upon them.

The Formation of a Sense of Personal Identity

It is generally accepted that the earliest stages of infancy are of paramount importance in building up a sense of trust, security and attachment (for example, Erikson, 1963; Bowlby 1969; Howe, 1995). The development of secure attachment is considered vital in providing a secure base from which a child can explore and for the development of self-esteem (e.g. Bowlby, 1969). Clarke and Clarke (1976) and others suggest that there is room in our multi-cultural society for a variety of acceptable patterns of attachment between young children and their families, and that even infants are capable of making deep attachments to several significant people (Schaffer, 1990).

Erikson's theories on identity have been particularly influential in the mainstream psychoanalytical tradition of child development (1959, 1963, 1968, 1980). In his classic *Eight Ages of Man* (1963) he postulated a series of stages of psychosocial development, the achievement of which is dependent on having progressed sequentially and satisfactorily from the previous stage. If the fundamental stage of 'basic trust' is not properly established in the first year of life, he said, then progression to the subsequent stages (e.g. autonomy, initiative, industry and identity) is impaired:

> A lasting ego-identity cannot begin to exist without the trust of the first oral stage; it cannot be completed without a promise of fulfilment which from the dominant image of adulthood reaches down into the baby's beginnings and which, by the tangible evidence of social health, creates at every step of childhood and adolescence an accruing sense of ego strength (Erikson, 1963, p. 238).

In Eriksonian theory, identification with, and incorporation of, the roles and values of key figures in the child's life takes place at every stage. During adolescence, the individual retains some of the earlier childhood identifications and rejects others in line with developing interests, abilities and values. The key task of adolescence, Erikson says, is the achievement of 'wholeness', or a 'sense of inner identity' through:

> ... a progressive continuity between that which [the young person] has come to be during the long years of childhood and that which he promises to become in the anticipated future; between that which he conceives himself to be and that which he perceives others to see in him and to expect of him. Individually speaking identity includes but is more than, the sum of all successive identifications of those earlier years when the child wanted to be, and was often forced to become, like the person he depended on. Identity is a unique product which now meets a crisis to be solved only in new identifications with age mates and with figures outside the family (1968, p. 87).

Resolution of this 'crisis' leads to: 'a more final self-definition, to irreversible role patterns, and thus to commitments for life' (Erikson, 1959, p 74). It gives a feeling of 'being at home in one's body, a sense of knowing where one is going' (p. 127). Erikson claims that this sense of personal identity is essential to be able to manage situations of crisis and difficulty in the future.

Erikson's theory emphasises the importance of the same two themes which Thoburn (1988) noted in the research studies of children growing up apart from their birth families – those of continuity and a sense of identity. Both psychoanalytical theory and research evidence support the notion that these factors are crucial to the development of self-esteem in the child and adult.

Marcia (1980) was influential in facilitating a means of measuring the achievement of a sense of identity. Research studies by Marcia and others have fairly consistently demonstrated a connection between the establishment of a clear sense of personal identity and a lower incidence of mental ill-health or emotional disturbance (for example, Howard and Kubis, 1964; Marcia, 1967, 1980; Stark and Traxler, 1974). Research has also associated identity achievement with high self-esteem, a greater sense of purpose in life, and heightened senses of self-responsibility and control (for example Adams and Shea, 1979; Read, Adams and Dobson, 1984). It should be pointed out however that some of this research, and the 'Eriksonian' approach generally, has been criticised by feminists such as Gilligan (1982) for its heavy reliance on research by men about men and its extrapolation from these findings to women. Others have also criticised the predominantly white, North American (as well as male) bias of this research (for example, Shweder and Bourne, 1982).

A further challenge to traditional ideas of identity formation has come from deconstructionists such as Derrida. They dispute the very notion that such a process is bounded by 'points of origin or conclusion' (Derrida, 1978, p. 226). They remind us that the development of a sense of identity is a dynamic process which continues throughout the life-cycle, and has social as well as individual meanings. Considerable evidence exists in childcare research of links between awareness of origins and identity achievement, though this is often related to adoption. There is a range of opinion as to the extent to which children's needs can be met by information alone, or whether continuing contact with birth parents is desirable. McWhinnie (1994) for example, tends to the former view, but Brodzinsky et al. (1992) show that children's information needs should be seen from a developmental perspective, so it is helpful to have on-going access to sources of information to be able to answer different questions as children grow older. Other research has shown that where children retain contact with their families of origin, they are more likely to acquire a clearer self-concept and more positive self-esteem (Fratter, 1994; Ryburn, 1994). Thoburn (1988, p. 48) concludes:

> All studies of children who are unable to be brought up by their natural parents strongly support the view that two essential elements in enhancing the well-being of such children are a sense of continuity in belonging to a family of which the child feels him or herself fully attached (usually referred to as a sense of permanence), and a sense of identity which is best achieved by continued contact with important people from the past.

The Social Identity of Those who Grow Up Apart from their Family of Origin

> The child who does not grow up with his own biological parents, who does not even know them or anyone of his own blood, is an individual who has lost the thread of family continuity. A deep identification with our forebears, as experienced originally in the mother-child relationship, gives us our most fundamental security. Every adopted child, at some point in his development, has been deprived of his primitive mother. This trauma and the severing of the individual from his racial antecedents lie at the core of what is peculiar to the psychology of the adopted child (Clothier, 1943).

Clothier referred to the 'psychology of the adopted child', while Brodzinsky et al. (1990) and others have described an 'adoptive identity'. It is possible to distil from the literature certain characteristics which adoptees share with those who grew up in care, but which distinguish them from their peers, giving this group a distinctive social identity. These include:

* experience of stigma;
* 'genealogical bewilderment'; and
* experience of separation and loss.

While the significance of separation and loss was examined in chapter 3, the first two characteristics are considered below.

Stigma

Secrecy and stigma have been recurrent themes throughout the history of childcare for children who grow up apart from their birth parents. Goffman (1963) developed the concept of 'spoiled identity' to signify the impact of stigma; groups may be perceived as 'inferior' or 'bad' simply because they are different. The 'differences' of those growing up in care are frequently all too visible. Children may attract attention because of a different surname from their foster carers, or from the necessity for statutory visits from social workers; from difficulties in accounting for the absence of parents or siblings, transport in vehicles with distinctive identifying logos, and so on. Those with a different skin colour to their carers are even more readily identified as 'not belonging'.

In Goffman's analysis, the perception of others affects the image we develop of ourselves. Thus, the negative perceptions within society of those outside the 'normal' family situation contribute towards their social identity. He addresses an aspect particularly relevant to those acquiring information about themselves and their origins later in life, when they may then become aware of stigmatisation for the first time. They then have to reorganise their 'view of the past' and re-identify themselves. This he says leads to a 'special likelihood of developing disapproval of self' (Goffman, 1963).

'Genealogical Bewilderment'

> Background knowledge of one's family is like babyfood – it is literally fed to a person as part of the normal nourishment that builds up his (or her) mental and emotional structure and helps the person to become acquainted with what he (or she) is so that he can seize his inheritance for himself (Kornitzer, 1971).

The term 'genealogical bewilderment' describes the state of confusion and uncertainty said to be experienced by the child (or adult) 'who either has no knowledge of his natural parents or only uncertain knowledge of them' (Sants, 1965, p. 32) Sants argues from a psychoanalytical approach, based especially on the work of Klein (1948, 1959), that this state fundamentally undermines the security, and thus the mental health, of the afflicted person. Clinical experience showed him that preoccupation with seeking clues to one's heritage often became an obsession, with the searcher believing that 'all their troubles would be solved by a solution to this one' (p. 33)

Sants illustrates the plight of the 'genealogically deprived' with the Hans Anderson story of the Ugly Duckling. He describes how the swan in the story is deprived of knowledge of the swan's genealogy by being hatched in a duck's family. He is rejected because he cannot do what the others in his foster family (a cat and a hen) can do because of his different genetic endowment. Because his foster parents did not know his genealogy they failed to recognise his skills or envisage his potential. The ugly duckling needed to identify with others like himself to feel that he belonged. When he finally saw his mature image, he was able to do this and identify himself successfully – and happily – as a swan.

Sants also discusses the significance of 'ancestor worship'. He suggests that some incorporation of our ancestors into our self-image is normal, and therefore being unable to achieve this through ignorance would appear to be 'incompatible with the secure self-image' (p. 39) Furthermore, he relates 'genealogical bewilderment' to the Oedipus myth, suggesting that anxieties about unknowingly committing incest may, consciously or unconsciously, play a role in the 'need to know' our genealogy.

It is suggested by several writers including Sants that awareness of resemblances is a particularly important aspect of knowledge of one's genealogy. Triseliotis (1973) for example, cited the importance for his respondents of finding out physical details of their birth parents in developing their own self body-image (p. 152). Sandler (1961) found that lack of resemblance could severely hamper 'a child's capacity to identify with his parents in order to reinforce any feeling he may have of belonging as the result of loving care' (p. 36)

Lifton (1988), writing about adoptees, points out the adverse impact of the combination of ignorance of origins together with the negative messages received and internalised about the birth parents. The taboos often placed upon asking questions about origins magnify 'the horrors of that unspeakable calamity that is buried in the past' (p. 40)

Cultural and Racial Identity

In looking at the significance of tracing one's origins, a distinction has already been drawn between personal and social identity. However one's identity is also generally considered to be derived from wider contexts, including race, gender, religion and culture. Indeed, many argue that race is a primary determinant of identity (for example, Dummet, 1973; Husband, 1986).

Issues of race and culture have received increasing attention in child welfare since around the early 1980s. The 1989 Children Act (Section 22) requires that due consideration be given, in placing children, to 'the child's religious persuasion, racial origin and cultural and linguistic background'. The Association of Black Social Workers and Allied Professionals has been particularly influential in this area, arguing against the practice of placing children transracially. They argue that an affirmation of pride in common roots provides protection against racism, and only black families can teach coping mechanisms to overcome the emotional damage of racism. However, the vast majority of black and mixed race adults who grew up in the period of this study experienced either transracial foster placements or care in residential establishments which were staffed predominantly by white carers. This begs a number of pertinent questions:

- What is the impact upon racial identity of transracial placement?
- How is this affected by knowledge, or ignorance, of one's heritage?
- What are the necessary conditions to create a positive sense of racial identity?

There has been considerable research upon these issues, both from the USA, and more recently, from the UK. However its evidence is frequently conflicting and open to criticism from various quarters. For example, research by Bagley and Young (1979) and Gill and Jackson (1983) in the UK, and by Simon and Altstein (1977, 1981) in the US showed that the majority of transracially adopted children in their studies (most research being focused on adoption) had little contact with their own racial group. Many 'misidentified' themselves as white, and showed a preference for 'whiteness'. However, most studies also reported above average adjustment, educational achievement and self-esteem in these same children. The different interpretations of these findings are discussed by Tizard and Phoenix (1994). They suggest that 'misidentifications' may have been more to do with black children's internalisation of racism and consequent low self-esteem.

It is pointed out by Small (1986) that none of these studies follows the children into adulthood, therefore there is a lack of knowledge of the longer-term impact of growing up in a transracial setting. One useful exception is Shekleton (1990), which describes the experiences and feelings of a group of transracially adopted adults who contacted the Post-Adoption Centre. Key issues for them included:

- discomfort with their body image which permeated their adult lives;
- coping with denial of difference by their adoptive parents, particularly in the case of light-complexioned individuals of mixed parentage;
- feelings of isolation, leading to either self-rejection or parental rejection;
- preoccupation with thoughts and fantasies about birth-parents especially in adolescence;
- constant readjustment of self-image through life, and feelings of alienation; and
- reluctance to involve agencies for fear of being seen as dysfunctional.

Although evidence from the literature is inconclusive, it seems reasonable to suppose that adults who were transracially placed as children may be more strongly motivated to seek knowledge about their origins where this has been lacking, in order to address their particular needs to achieve a strong sense of racial and cultural identity. However, the findings above from the Post-Adoption Centre (1990) indicate that this group may also find it especially difficult to seek help to find the information they desire.

Conclusion to Part 1

One of the most striking features to emerge from this review of the literature is the extent to which adoption has held its place in the limelight to the detriment of all other forms of substitute care. In all aspects of the debate about secrecy v. openness, severance v. continuity, separation, identity and self-esteem in child-care, attention to adoption predominates. On the specific question addressed by this study the contrast is even more marked. As chapter 2 shows, there have been several research studies of significance into the impact of the legal provision under which adoptees may since 1975 (in England and Wales) gain access to their original birth certificates (e.g. Triseliotis 1973; Leeding, 1977; Day, 1979; Haimes and Timms, 1985; Walby and Simons, 1990). There have been no major studies looking specifically at those who grew up in care and requested access to their personal records.

I would suggest several reasons for this difference. Firstly, the historic changes brought about by the implementation of Section 26 of the 1975 Children Act heralded a new era in adoption and generated a minor explosion of research interest. Secondly since provision for adoptees wishing to gain access to their birth records is enshrined in legislation, procedures for accessing this service are clearly defined, both for the adoptee and for the would-be researcher. By contrast, there is no clear-cut or consistent route for the non-adoptee who wishes to explore his origins. Procedures for gaining access to personal records vary widely between individual local authorities and voluntary organisations. The service is not generally well-publicised, it is rarely provided by specifically designated staff, and appears often to be regarded as a low priority.

Thirdly, perhaps the lack of a clear-cut identity for the group which this study addresses deters academic attentions. Those who grow up in care not only lack the distinctive legal status of adoptees they even lack a universally accepted name or title to identify them as members of a group.

Much of our knowledge, then, of the process of searching for origins, is derived from adoption research. The various studies have explored similar themes – the motivation for the search, characteristics of searchers, their aims and expectations and the outcomes of their searches. Some studies have looked at the experiences of those whose searches have led beyond the acquisition of mere knowledge about origins and on to reunions with adoptive parents or others (e.g. Parish and Cotton, 1988; Sachdev, 1992; Feast, 1992; Feast and Howe, 1997).

So what is the relevance of adoption research in this field for the 'searchers' who grew up in care? Because of the lack of knowledge of the latter group, comparative analysis of the impact of acquiring information about one's heritage is not possible. One can only speculate upon possible differences in impact from an analysis of the features of the two groups.

In chapter 4 it was seen that the two key elements in achieving a sense of self-worth in adulthood were generally considered to be a sense of permanence, or belonging, and a sense of identity which comes from continuing contact with, or at least knowledge of, people from one's past (e.g. Erikson, 1959; Thoburn, 1988). Whilst the extent of personal understanding about origins varies considerably amongst both adoptees and non-adoptees, it is the existence of a sense of permanence, of continuity, which distinguishes the former from the latter. As Hill et al. (1989) demonstrated, even those who grew up in long-term foster homes felt a significant qualitative difference between their form of care and adoption: 'Adoption was identified with continuity of care, permanence and security' (p. 137).

One may therefore conclude that those who experienced several changes of carer felt a proportionately greater sense of insecurity and lack of any sense of belonging or continuity. This is borne out by the research examined in chapter 3, indicating, in general, a significantly greater sense of well-being and functioning in adulthood for those growing up adopted than for those who experienced other forms of care (e.g. Triseliotis and Hill, 1990). Aldgate (1988) also highlighted the way in which the quality of care received after separation significantly influenced the impact of the separation and loss itself upon the individual.

If those who grew up in care are significantly lacking (in comparison with adoptees, let alone the rest of the population) in one of the key components for achieving a sense of self-worth in adulthood (i.e. a sense of permanence), then it would seem reasonable to suppose that a greater sense of importance might attach to achieving the other vital factor, a clear sense of identity, deriving primarily from an understanding of one's roots.

PART 2
THE STUDY

5 Methodology

Introduction

In the introduction to the study, I explained how my fascination with this topic was triggered by a television documentary about the work of Barnardo's and subsequently being appointed to a new job as a social worker in Barnardo's After Care Section, working with adults who wanted to find out about their family background and time in care. I wanted to gain a better understanding of what it meant to these people to find out about their origins later in life, and to go beyond the initial reactions which I witnessed in my social work role. In starting my research at much the same time as my new job, I felt I would be approaching the subject with an open mind, hopefully lessening the dangers of prejudging the nature or the outcome of the phenomenon I was researching – what Lofland and Lofland (1984) referred to as 'starting where you are'. I was primarily concerned to further my own, and others', theoretical understanding of the topic, but also hoped that the research might have 'real world value' (Robson, 1993), leading to some tangible and useful ends.

Planning the Study

Both professional experience and the literature study were used to develop what Strauss and Corbin (1990) called 'theoretical sensitivity'. The advantages and disadvantages of various alternative research methodologies were considered, and a broadly qualitative approach was chosen, using semi-structured interviews, with a sample of adults who had seen their records through Barnardo's After Care Section (further details below). An outline of the study was prepared to enable necessary consents to be obtained (Appendix 1). Formal consent was sought from potential participants in the research, giving careful consideration to ethical aspects of the study, particularly issues of confidentiality.

Methodology and Epistemology

The research question centred around the impact of receiving information about family background and origins upon adults who had grown up in Barnardo's care. In order to penetrate the surface of the topic, the scope of the research was narrowed to consider only adults who grew up in care (and then, specifically in Barnardo's care), rather than all who were separated from their families of origin.

In selecting a methodology for the research, firstly the most appropriate 'technical fit' of method to the question addressed, and secondly epistemological issues were considered, on the basis that 'how one goes about doing research is intimately connected to what is going on in the world, how one sees the world and how one sees social work' (Trinder, 1996).

The choice of research strategy was influenced by the purpose of the enquiry, which was primarily exploratory. I wanted to find out more about the phenomena of adults seeking information about their origins, to seek new insights and to understand what these findings meant. My aim was to seek the subjective meanings which these adults attached to the particular events and experiences in their lives, and this led me towards the qualitative methods of data collection.

Lack of empirical rigour or lack of analysis in the interests of obtaining subjective experience, can lay qualitative research open to criticism. One option might have been simply allowing informants to give their oral histories without imposing any analysis or interpretation. This would still have ignored the role played by the researcher's perspective, 'cultural lens', gender and so on. These epistemological dilemmas are difficult to resolve satisfactorily. However, use of the grounded theory approach provides a qualitative research method which is nevertheless rigorous and systematic, in that it:

> ... uses a systematic set of procedures to develop an inductively derived grounded theory about a phenomenon. The research findings consist a theoretical formulation of the reality under investigation, rather than consisting of a set of numbers, or a group of loosely related themes. Through this methodology the concepts and relationships among them are not only generated but they are also provisionally tested (Strauss and Corbin 1990).

Interviews were selected as the most effective research method for eliciting individual perceptions and feelings and allowing in-depth, open-ended responses. I wanted to understand each individual's experience in its own right, rather than as a means of understanding the population from which it was drawn.

Access

Permission was sought to interview people who had seen their childcare records from Barnardo's. Gaining an understanding of the historical perspective of Barnardo's work was to prove very relevant. I was not primarily attempting to evaluate the service provided, nor seeking feedback about the performance of social work staff, although this might be offered.

All the work of identifying and contacting participants, interviewing and subsequent analysis and writing up was undertaken by myself in my own time and at my own expense.

Ethical Issues

The codes of conduct of both the British Sociological Association ('Statement of Ethical Practice') and the British Psychological Society (Robson, 1993) were used to address potential ethical concerns or conflicts of interest. An initial letter was sent to all potential participants explaining the aims of the research, my credentials and conditions regarding confidentiality. Despite the personal and sensitive nature of the topic, participants seemed to have few qualms about confidentiality. This however in no way reduced the responsibility to be vigilant on their behalf. In writing up the study I have quoted participants verbatim, but have changed names and some identifying details unless specifically requested not to.

Data Collection

Within the constraints of limited time and resources, it was aimed to interview 12–15 people, selected from those who had seen their records via Barnardo's After Care Section at least one year previously. It was hoped that participants would have had time to reflect on the experience and impact of gaining this information, and to allow for subsequent developments related to this, such as tracing relatives or impact upon the health or relationships of the person who had seen their records. Not wanting so much time to have elapsed that the experience of gaining information was but a distant memory, I selected those who had viewed their files within the last four years. Most of the sample had seen their records between one and two years previously.

The study was not seeking to achieve representativeness or statistically significant information, but rather seeking to show individual perceptions and feelings about an experience. The sampling strategy was therefore purposeful rather than random, and most closely accorded with, what Patton (1990) calls maximum variation sampling. A balance of gender, age and race in participants was sought. Anybody with severe mental health problems or who was currently undergoing counselling or treatment was omitted to reduce the risk of causing additional distress to those people.

Twenty potential participants were approached before obtaining 12 positive responses. As interviewing progressed, it appeared likely that these 12 would yield sufficiently rich and varied data without the need for larger numbers. The age of respondents ranged from 42 to 74, with a mean age of 58. There were seven men and five women, all of whom were white except one black man of mixed race. Two had disabilities. Although not seeking a statistically representative sample of all Barnardo's clients who had viewed their records, this appeared to be a fair reflection of this population. It reflects the priority given since the 1995 influx of requests to older people wanting to see their records, from a waiting list with a much wider spread of ages.

A taped interview was conducted with each participant lasting one to one-and-a-half hours. These were semi-structured, using an interview guide (Appendix 2).

Data Analysis

The grounded theory approach as developed by Glaser and Strauss (1967) was used. All interview tapes were transcribed, each one generating new material.

Having identified and conceptualised categories in the data through basic coding, the next stage using grounded theory was to search for relationships and themes within the open codes to create higher level, or 'axial' codes. The aim was to build theory 'from the bottom up'. This process accorded with Strauss and Corbin's definition of coding:

Coding represents the operations by which data are broken down, conceptualised, and put back together in new ways. It is the central process by which theories are built from the data (Strauss and Corbin, 1990, p. 57).

From the development of the higher level codes, and via an iterative process of constantly going back over the transcripts and checking out emerging theory and modifying ideas, a 'main storyline' gradually emerged. This led directly towards the broad chapter headings for the write-up of the study, as seen in Part 2. A typology was developed from among the participants to demonstrate the connections between their childhood experiences and the impact of seeing their records. This became a major theme in the study.

Review

This was a small, qualitative research study using semi-structured, focused interviews to explore the impact upon adults who grew up in Barnardo's care of gaining access to their childcare records. Purposeful sampling was used to select a sample of 12 cases to explore the feelings and perceptions of the individuals concerned. Grounded theory was the chosen method of data analysis. The findings are presented in the following chapters.

6 Introduction to the Findings

In order to explain the context in which the study was undertaken, some background information about the work of the After Care Section of Barnardo's is given, before presenting the findings of the study. The following information is extracted from *Revealing Histories* (Bradford, 1994).

- Between 1886 and 1975 Barnardo's cared for 350,000 children in long term residential settings and a variety of foster placements throughout the UK.
- A family background history was prepared for the majority of the children admitted to Barnardo's. The children were photographed on admission and later on leaving care. We have half a million photographs of the children.
- The early records from 1870–1941 consist of large registers with copper plate handwriting including photographs of the children and mostly administrative information. From 1941 onwards more information was written about the children themselves. From the 1960s onwards there is a great deal more information. Most of Barnardo's files are now on microfilm.
- Files frequently contain third party information (which must be extracted). Admission histories were marked 'strictly confidential'. Staff or foster parents would not know the contents. There is concern about the language used in files, e.g. 1951: 'Mother is a big dirty-looking woman of weak mentality. She is crafty, abusive, foul-mouthed and entirely amoral'.
- 1,500 inquiries are received per year. The age range of inquirers is 23 up to 102. A large proportion of inquirers are aged 40–60 years.

Aims and Objectives of the service:

1. to provide information and counselling for former clients about their family background;
2. to help clients trace birth parents and siblings and act as intermediaries where possible;

3. to enable clients to make sense of their care experience by providing information;
4 to provide counselling on any of the following issues: loss, separation from siblings, sexual abuse, physical abuse, racism, incest, extramarital parentage, putative fathers.

There has been a gradual move towards greater openness of access to records for After Care clients in recent years. Some of those interviewed for this study received only a summary of their file contents – an expurgated, and often sanitised version of their lives. Only since 1996 has it been possible for clients to see their entire files if they wish, subject to the extraction of third party material and to the exercise of 'duty of care' considerations, and to retain copies of material they have viewed. Most people now therefore receive an admission history, a photo or two of themselves, dates and locations of their placements, and brief details of family contacts whilst in care. Files sometimes additionally contain reports of welfare visits to foster homes, annual progress reviews, correspondence with birth families or internal documents regarding decisions or arrangements for placements.

It is also relevant to note that the showing in 1995 (and again in 1997) of the BBC documentaries, *Barnardo's Children*, had a major impact on the work of the After Care Section. Over 4,000 requests for information were received in the immediate aftermath of the 1995 films, plus many more over the following months. Despite doubling the numbers of staff in the Section, a lengthy waiting list was inevitable. Decisions were taken to prioritise requests from the elderly, those with serious medical conditions and others with exceptional circumstances, such as those who have alleged abuse in care. It was agreed that such sensitive information must be imparted in a personal interview, and often more than one session would be required; a high standard of practice is very time consuming, but is a commitment reflecting Barnardo's sense of responsibility towards its former children. However this meant that many enquirers, including several of those in this study, had to wait months or even years before receiving their information. This is an issue of great concern and under constant review in the Section, but needs to be taken into account when examining respondents' reactions to the service they received.

When people were interviewed for this study about the impact of getting their information, everybody talked, not only about their current feelings and situation, but also to a great extent about their childhoods. As I attempted to make sense of what I was hearing, I came to realise that looking back to the past had a significance far beyond mere reminiscing. It was not possible to separate out the childhood experiences and memories from feelings about themselves in the present, and it became clear that the impact of gaining access to their files could never be fully understood without an understanding of the person's feelings about their past. This gave new meaning to the social work principle of 'starting with where the client is coming from', rather than imposing a worker-led agenda.

The presentation of findings in Part 2 therefore reflects this important point: the impact of receiving information cannot be properly understood without first understanding where the person is coming from. The next chapter, 'Looking Back to Childhood', addresses this area. It explains how people saw themselves as children growing up in care, their experiences of life in residential care or foster homes, memories and feelings about their birth families, about loss and separation and about the importance of the blood tie. It describes and analyses their attitudes towards Barnardo's and their struggles to achieve a sense of identity as they grew up. The feelings expressed and memories recalled are of course from the adult's standpoint, looking back and reflecting upon the meaning of their past. The process of reflection upon the past triggered further memories, sometimes long-forgotten or buried, and the nature of these recollections shed further light on how the past had shaped these people.

In chapter 8, 'Motivation for Seeking Information', I examine why people wanted to seek out information about their past – what triggered their request at that point in their lives, their differing motivations and emotions, and their hopes and fears about what they might find. I sought to explore whether – or how – these factors might be linked to people's experiences and feelings about the past.

Finally, in the light of these findings, chapter 9 explores 'The Impact of Receiving Information'. Having discovered just what people found in their records, I enquired whether it had met, or perhaps exceeded their expectations; what they felt about the way in which the information-sharing process had taken place, what emotions it had aroused and how people coped with those emotions. I also looked at whether reading their files led on to further searching or tracing and how all this affected those around the person. I then share the reflections of those who have been through this experience about how it has shaped their views of themselves, of Barnardo's, and of families, and explore how they have managed to make sense of the past.

7　Looking Back to Childhood

Experiences of Substitute Care

'Barnardo's Children' may have shared a certain distinctive corporate identity, but their experiences of growing up in care were far from uniform.

This study focuses on the majority of children cared for by Barnardo's who grew up in residential or foster homes. It was possible for a child to experience exclusively residential care or exclusively foster care, though not necessarily wholly within one establishment or home. However many experienced a variety of placements. Patterns of care impact on the quality of relationships experienced, and people's level of satisfaction with their care.

Within my sample, three distinctive groupings could be identified according to the nature of the care they received in childhood. Most sharply defined were the group I have referred to as the 'real families' – three out of the 12 interviewees. They had been removed in the first year of their lives from their birth families and placed by Barnardo's in long-term foster homes where they had stayed for most of their childhood. Although they had grown up in the full knowledge that they were not born into these families, they regarded them in every other sense as 'their family':

> My mother was my mother, I never class her now as Mrs C., I never thought of her as a foster mother though I knew she was. And nobody else was my mother (Jim, 55).

They achieved the sought-after 'family for life', and saw little need for, and felt little curiosity about, their birth families as they were growing up:

> That was still my home even when I got married and had my own family ... the kids all called her granny ... she was their granny (Mary, 58).

This group all expressed a high degree of satisfaction with, and gratitude towards, their substitute families. Pete (49) particularly appreciated what his white foster parents must have been through in fostering a black child in their rural community in the 1950s and 'what stick they must have had to take!':

> ... Not only do I love my foster mother but she's done so much for me and put
> herself out for me that I could never – my real mother could never replace that.
> That might sound a bit nasty but its just something she could never do.

The 'real families' group bore the most resemblance to adoptees, although
there were significant differences. In particular, Barnardo's widely-applied
policy of 'recalling' children from even the most stable of substitute family
situations at the age of 14 to learn a trade (boys), or be trained for a life in
'service' (girls) , meant that they could never forget that they were first and
foremost Barnardo's children.

The opposite extreme to the 'real families' group were the larger group
who could be termed 'rootless'. This comprised Ron (74), Alf (71), Fred (66),
Betty (59), June (56) and Ann (42). Like the 'real families', this group had
generally been in Barnardo's care from a very early age and had little or no
memory of living with their birth families. In contrast to the stability of the
'real families' group, for reasons which were seldom apparent, they had
experienced numerous moves in care. They described these as 'being shunted
around', or 'moved from pillar to post'. Where they had been 'boarded out'
with a family, it had either been such a transitory move, or an unhappy or
even abusive experience, that they had not put down any roots with that family,
and had not achieved a substitute family identity. Alf spoke of always feeling
the 'odd one out' in his foster family ...

> They had their own family, and, when you got older, you were the lackey, anyone
> doing the dirty deeds, you did it ... she did keep you well fed and clothed and
> that, they were getting paid so they had to didn't they? Whether they did it for
> the money or the love I don't know ...

Ann experienced years of physical and emotional abuse from what she
called her 'foster parents from hell' who both suffered from mental illness.
Vivid memories, long buried, came back to her as she talked:

> You know butter wrappers? She used to scrape butter wrappers like a raving
> lunatic. She used to scrape her fingers. I can remember having a nightdress
> with bunnies on it and I can remember the bunnies turning red where she splashed
> me with blood.

Her plight was eventually discovered and she was moved on to a residential
placement. Her troubles were not over here though. During weekend visits to
a social aunt and uncle she was sexually abused by the couple's teenage son.

Yet she says,

> I used to like going there. Although it must sound totally mad now, I knew that if I'd opened my mouth then, I'd have been back sitting in Barnardo's with all the other kids on a Sunday. I wouldn't have been able to watch Perry Mason on a Saturday night. And not to have to go to church three times a day which was a real result 'cos I hated church. I'd stand what he was doing to me rather than not be allowed to go.

Like Ann and several others, Alf had experienced both fostering and residential care, having spent time in one of Barnardo's naval training schools. Although the regime there was tough, it was the loneliness of having nobody to call his own which Alf found hardest to cope with:

> The most hurtful thing was, they used to put this notice on the board every day, about a month before the Christmas and summer holidays, about the people they've heard from, parents or foster parents who say they want their children home for the holidays. So you used to run there every day, have a look at that board, but my name was never on there, never once, so you had to spend all your holidays in the school.

For a couple of interviewees, disabilities had precluded them in the 1940s from being deemed suitable for a family placement. One of these praised the specialist care she received in one home where she was 'very happy'. Unfortunately however this was only one of many placements she experienced. Others were less happy:

> You didn't get the individual attention. There were a lot of times I used to cry. I asked the matron, where was my mummy, why couldn't I go home to my mummy, and I was told she'd died.

She later found this to be untrue. This woman met her mother several years later, but was once again rejected when she found herself single and pregnant. Another interviewee said of residential care:

> I was lonely ... even if you're in a Home, children and people caring for you, you're still lonely, still feel very, sort of, rejected ... you do get an awful feeling you're not wanted.

In varying degrees the 'rootless' group had gone through childhood lacking any close attachments to caring adults, whether blood relations or otherwise.

This was poignantly illustrated by Ron who described how he had decided to change his name because he hated it:

> Well I thought it wouldn't matter anyway 'cos no-one would be concerned, 'cos there was nobody out there anyway, so I might as well have a name that I got on with!

He added that he had never had any control over his destiny before, but this was something he was proud of doing for himself. With remarkable stoicism, this group recalled memories which were predominantly sad and dominated by a pervasive sense of loss.

Somewhere between the extremes of the 'rootless' and the 'real families' lay the third group, which I termed the 'rescued' group. This group, comprising Tom (62), Bill (63), and Jean (45) had spent their early childhood with their birth families, but had been removed from this environment and admitted to Barnardo's care because of neglect or abuse. Perhaps because they were older at the time of admission – between the ages of seven and 12 years old – all three in this category went into residential care, but managed to remain in one stable placement for all or most of their time in care. Jean, for example, had been able to remain together with her seven siblings in the same establishment, which was very important to her.

Whilst tending to lack close one-to-one attachments in their residential care homes, this group nevertheless compared their new lives very favourably with their old ones from which they saw themselves as being 'rescued'. Tom had entered Barnardo's after his father's death, which had left him and his siblings in the care of his mentally ill mother. He explained:

> I felt protected in Barnardo's. We were better off education-wise, and mentally healthier ... we were growing up in a stronger world than a world dominated by a woman who really only wanted us out of the way.

For them the peer group assumed an important role, and so too did the concept of belonging to the 'Barnardo's family'. Bill described his life in one of Barnardo's trade schools for boys as 'the happiest days of my life', and said,

> They gave me everything. Before I went into Barnardo's, we used to get hit with the stiletto heel of my mother's shoe ... the last time I saw my sister, I can always remember her having a split lip where my mother had wacked her, she was 13 months old ...

Even now, the annual reunions of the 'old boys' from his Home are the high points of Bill's social calendar.

In conclusion, the interviewees' descriptions of their childhood in care encompassed a wide range of experiences and emotions. These fell roughly into the three groups outlined, each group having a distinctive outlook on what care meant to them. In examining the rest of the findings of this study, I wanted to see whether these groups shared other characteristics or views, and if so, whether these also influenced the impact upon them of gaining access to their records.

Feelings about Birth Families

The feelings of the people I interviewed about their birth families seemed potentially highly relevant to understanding the impact upon them of finding out more about their origins. All had been severed from their birth families during childhood. For all except the 'rescued' group this had taken place during their first year of life. Apart from the rescued group, who had spent a significant period with their birth families, none of the others had grown up with any contact with their birth parents during their time in Barnardo's, and had little or no information about their origins either until adulthood. A few had some knowledge of having siblings but had been separated from them at an early stage and had lost contact with them. Pete was an exception in that he had been placed in his long-term foster home with his twin sister, and they had remained together throughout childhood.

The extent of this severance from birth families may seem surprising in the light of current policies which emphasise the importance of maintaining contact with birth families. I have no way of quantifying how common this scenario was for Barnardo's children generally. It may be that my sample, who had mostly been referred to me by social workers, gives undue prominence to this group because of their especial interest in acquiring information about their origins, coming as they did from a baseline of almost total ignorance. However during the period when this group grew up (1920s–50s), Barnardo's policies emphasised the 'fresh start' approach, and felt children often needed to be protected from their birth families. This meant that even where birth families may have endeavoured to maintain contact, at least by letter, Barnardo's censorship sometimes resulted in children being kept unaware of their family's interest.

In this section, I look at people's attitudes towards their birth families and the significance they attached to the blood tie. I tried to find out whether their attitudes followed any pattern – whether they were linked to the typology of the 'real families', 'rootless' and 'rescued' groups identified earlier, and in particular, whether the quality of the substitute care they received in Barnardo's was linked to their feelings about birth families.

Since reading their files, around half the people I interviewed had had some form of reunion with a birth relative – in every case a sibling rather than a parent, a factor probably related to the ages of the group. Their views about birth families are obviously coloured by these experiences, which sometimes changed previously held feelings towards their families.

I found that the group termed the 'real families' shared a common and distinctive attitude towards their birth families. All three members of this group (Mary, Jim and Pete) were emphatic that their 'real' parents were their day-to-day, psychological parents – in Mary's words, 'the ones who were loving us, looking after us when we were sick' and so on. Of her biological mother, Mary said,

> I always call her my supposed-to-be-mother! Well, she isn't my mother, is she? She only had me, I don't know her.

Even when, as adults, two members of this group, Mary and Jim, are traced by their siblings, their feelings towards these birth relatives range from indifference to somewhat muted pleasure:

> When I was 40, one of my 'real' sisters turned up on the doorstep. She said, 'I'm your sister Margery'. And I said, 'Are you?' And I didn't feel anything. I just didn't feel anything. And they say blood's thicker than water. To me it's not, not in that respect, no, not at all (Mary, 58).

Pete (49) decided not to try and trace his mother. He is very close even today to his twin sister who was placed with him, but the absence of his biological parents in his life was of little importance to him:

> My real mother would never take the place of my foster mother, never. So that would be the only hurt if I met my real mother – whether I would feel I had to give her something that I couldn't give her. I would probably feel I had to give her more love than I could.

Neither Jim nor Pete felt any anger or animosity towards their birth parents for having given them up; they accepted that there had been weaknesses or mistakes made in the past but showed understanding of their parents' fallibility, if not perhaps approval. Mary, however, was aware of having been physically abused by her birth mother – and had the scars to show for it – and was openly hostile towards her. Mary very much hoped to discover that her father was a more sympathetic character than her mother.

I found other examples of where one parent was known to have been an abuser or in other ways appeared to have been a 'bad' parent, then there was a strong urge on the part of the son or daughter to believe that the other parent was 'good'. Perhaps this was an understandable desire to be the inheritor of at least some 'good' genes, or perhaps this was a protective mechanism to promote self-esteem. Or perhaps what I witnessed was, in psychoanalytical terms, 'splitting', where someone is unable to integrate both good and bad elements within one individual (especially a parent) and can only see them as all good or all bad. I found this featured particularly strongly in all three members of the 'rescued' group.

Jean had suffered years of sexual abuse from her birth father and hated him to the extent that she was unable to say the word 'father' in our interview without retching on every occasion. She was admitted to Barnardo's on the death of her mother. It was painful to her to try to understand why her mother had not protected her from this abuse, and this was a major motivation for her in seeking access to her files. And yet she says, when she was a child:

> My mother was the be-all of my existence. You couldn't have said a wrong thing about my mother. I always thought of her as a brilliant mum, and loved her to distraction.

Similarly Tom talked of rejection and neglect by his mentally ill mother, but expressed strongly contrasting sentiments about his father, who died when Tom was 11:

> Dad was the icon of my existence. Next to God there wasn't anybody greater. If he said to me when he came home on army leave, I'm going to take you to the pictures, if there was six feet of snow I'd go. He was the be-all and end-all as far as I was concerned.

For Bill, the 'splitting' process is both between his birth mother and his birth father, and also between his birth parents and his substitute parents, whom he regards as Barnardo's. Bill recalls his mother, who was imprisoned for cruelty and neglect of her children, and says even if she were still alive today he would never speak to her again. His father, though, he feels tried his

best for them under difficult circumstances. His attitude towards his father
seems to have relented since discovering from his files that his father had
made efforts to keep in touch while he was in care. In contrast though to the
venom directed towards his mother, Bill cannot sing the praises of Barnardo's
highly enough:

> I absolutely loved Barnardo's and all it stands for. I was in there 12 years and I
> can't think of one day that was bad ... I will never say a bad word about
> Barnardo's.

Inevitably, those who had good memories of birth parents they had lost
recalled an acute sense of loss and grief during their childhood. Others grieved
for the loss of parents they had never known. This was particularly true for
those who were unable to achieve close attachments with substitute carers –
the 'rootless' group.

It was common (but not universal) across the groups for people to assume,
in the face of ignorance about why they had come into Barnardo's care, that
they had been rejected by their birth parents. This was a source of hurt and
was sometimes expressed by anger or defiance:

> I had a letter from my mother when I was 18 and she wanted to meet me ... I
> wrote back and said, no, I didn't want to know her ... she didn't want me as a
> baby – she ain't having me now! (Mary).

> If they're not bothered with me after all these years, why should I suddenly
> look for them? (Fred).

But despite the hurt feelings, where no other close relationships took the
place of the birth family, there was much more ambivalence towards the lost
parents, and sometimes a most poignant longing to discover that someone
would one day want them, and that they might discover a more acceptable
explanation for their separation. June, for example, was removed from her
parents for cruelty as a baby and did not meet them again until late adolescence.
Despite repeatedly being let down and rejected by both parents over the ensuing
years, June was reluctant to condemn them wholeheartedly and persisted in
seeking justifications for their behaviour. Her reactions – for example, when
her mother declined a request to visit the young June in hospital when she
was thought to be dying – were of resigned acceptance – 'so, that was that!'.
One of the few times she expressed emotions, she spoke of being left feeling
'empty again'.

Ron (74), whose predominant recollection of his time in care was being 'shunted around' a succession of different placements, and knew nothing whatsoever about his birth family, told me:

> When you're younger, you've always got this idea that someone'll eventually come looking for you. But if they don't, that's it. That's the only thing you've got at the back of your mind.

When Ron approached Barnardo's for access to his family background information at the age of 72, he still nurtured a hope that it was not too late to find his mother. This is not uncommon. As a social worker in Barnardo's I have worked with an 83 year old who hoped that his unknown mother may have been a young girl when she abandoned him on a railway station at birth and therefore might still be alive and traceable. The yearning for a lost mother does not appear to vanish with age.

In the final chapter in this section I look further at the area of tracing and reunions with birth relatives. As may be expected from these feelings expressed about their birth families, the desire to find birth relatives was strongest amongst those who had least in the way of attachments, i.e. the 'rootless' group. Having nothing or no-one else in their lives, they were the most prepared to overlook past rejections and misdemeanours by their families in the hope of a belated chance of a happy reunion.

One further aspect related to birth families which emerged from my interviews was the very high value placed by almost everyone on achieving quality family relationships in their own and subsequent generations. Despite their very mixed experiences of 'family life' as children, a happy and stable family of their own was an important goal for virtually everyone. This had not always been easy to achieve, but a high proportion of the people I interviewed, even among the 'rootless' group appeared to have stable marriages and children (and sometimes grandchildren) of whom they were extremely proud.

In conclusion then, there appeared to be a significant link between people's attitudes towards their birth families and their care experiences in Barnardo's. The blood tie was valued least highly by those who had enjoyed satisfactory substitute family care. It was the psychological parent and not the biological parent who was important to them.

Those who had had bad experiences of parenting by their birth parents were generally happy with the care they received in residential homes, and tended to value the support of their peer group as much as that of caring adults. The 'rescued' group had strong negative views about one parent (usually an abuser) and highly idealised views about the other parent. Those who perceived the absence of the birth family as a significant gap or loss in their lives – mostly the 'rootless' group – were more prepared to forgive the perpetrator and allow for the possibility of a better relationship in the future. On the one hand they felt the pain of rejection, real or assumed, by their birth families, but on the other hand, the hope of a possible happy reunion at some point in their lives featured strongly as a most desirable aspiration. To them, families represented closeness, belonging, and security and they felt the lack of these very deeply. Alf (71) summed it up when he said:

> When I first met my wife, her mum and dad took to me, and that was the first real family I had. My foster parents, they weren't family. I think that makes a lot of difference to you, family life. You know, you've never had one, and you treasure it more.

Attitudes Towards Barnardo's

> Once you're taken into Barnardo's, you belong to the Barnardo's family, and they don't tell you about anybody else (Alf).

By the 1950s, Barnardo's had begun to move towards helping children to stay with, or at least have contact with, their own families. But during the period when those interviewed were growing up in care, from the 1920s through to the 1950s, Barnardo's policy was generally to protect children from the presumed undesirable influences of their families, and to promote Barnardo's as their surrogate family. This was illustrated by Alf's situation:

> I was about 15 when they first told me I'd got a sister, and they sent me home on leave to meet her. She'd been fostered out and I'd been fostered out – about ten miles apart as the crow flies and we never knew anything about each other.

It was not deemed helpful or desirable to remind children of their past; instead they were encouraged to put the past behind them and 'look to the future'. Continued contact with Barnardo's into adulthood was encouraged, as was a due sense of gratitude to 'the Homes' for all they had done.

So how did this affect those to whom I spoke? I wondered whether they *did* regard Barnardo's as their family, whether they did feel grateful, and what they felt about Barnardo's approach to family contact and its policy of withholding information about family background.

As might be expected, those who felt happiest about their experience in care were most likely to view Barnardo's positively as an organisation. The most outspokenly enthusiastic was Bill (63), who clearly saw Barnardo's as a kind of knight in shining armour, rescuing him from the clutches of a cruel parent:

> What was the alternative for me in those circumstances, to going into Barnardo's, where would I be? I'd be what I was when I was five or six years of age, I'd be a street urchin. Now that could have led to anything.

Bill seemed to identify strongly with the notion of Barnardo's as his family, and it was very important to him that his own children and grandchildren understood and became part of this family. He enthused about his training school, Goldings, and their annual reunions:

> Awesome place it is, even now. We all (pointing to grandchildren) trek off to see the boys – old boys they are now, every year, probably 200–300 of us get back there – we all love it still.

Bill reacted to criticisms of Barnardo's much as a child might defend its parent from attack:

> I've seen such rubbish on TV. People whinge! I get so – I swear terrible – I hate it! They must have been in a different Barnardo's to me. I mean, they gave me everything. I could never repay them if I tried.

The other person who was almost as positive about Barnardo's was Pete (49). He also spent time at Goldings, despite spending most of his time in a long-term foster home:

> Apparently all Barnardo's boys did that, if they were fostered out or whatever, so I just went there and that was that. A lot of people said, god, its like being in an institution. But it wasn't. To me, it was a nice place to go ... so I've never regretted Barnardo's. At the end of the day, its done me no harm and I've always praised Barnardo's for that. My life is completely different from what it could have been. Its been perfect ... its been no problem.

Amongst those with experience of being fostered, either long or short term, it seemed to be commonly believed that being 'fostered out' was to 'come out of Barnardo's', even though they were still very much under the care and supervision of Barnardo's. Bill, for example, told me his sister 'wasn't in Barnardo's', but later said, 'she went into Barnardo's as a baby, then she was fostered, so she doesn't really know what Barnardo's is all about'.

In contrast to Bill who felt Barnardo's provided him with all the 'family' he could wish for, Ron (74) felt he had missed out on the very qualities that he regarded as essential to a sense of belonging:

> You never got close to anybody, because it wasn't their policy to do so … they were just concerned you weren't ill or anything.

For Pete and the rest of the 'real families' group, the fact that they knew very little about their family background as they grew up was not a problem; as Pete said, 'I'm not bothered, I'm quite happy as I am'. But for those in the 'rootless' group, the lack of a family caused a deep sense of loss, and when their attempts to find out were thwarted by Barnardo's , this was a major issue for them, and often a source of anger:

> I could not get any information. I tried in my early years to find out, as one does, and I just didn't get any response at all. Their policy was – no surrender! Wouldn't give you anything! (Ron).

> When you went in the Barnardo's Homes everything was censored and you didn't know anything and you weren't allowed to contact your relations at all. I just think at times they were cruel, I really do … you do feel angry, and the older you get, the more angry you become. You think, WHY! (Fred).

There was however some reluctance to express wholehearted criticism of Barnardo's, whether from a conflict of loyalties or perhaps for fear of offending me. For example, Alf said, 'I expect Barnardo's thought they were doing the right thing but, I still think that's cruel'.

Of the criticisms of Barnardo's, it was their policy of secrecy and severing family ties during the period concerned which drew the most comments. But while some praised the opportunities they had been given in care, others felt they had missed out, particularly in education. Ron told me:

> I was told one day I'd passed my scholarship, but I always think we were held back because we were who we were, because the very next day they told me I hadn't passed it. And I always thought that it was because we were Barnardo's children.

Ron felt a deep sense of injustice that his opportunities in life had been limited by Barnardo's – not just by their apparent unwillingness to pay for him to have further education but by their attitude, as he saw it, that Barnardo's children were somehow different, and by implication, inferior to their peers. How this impacted on the self-esteem and sense of identity of Ron and the others is examined below.

Sense of Identity

The literature on this subject suggested that those who grow up in care without contact with their families of origin are likely to share a social identity characterised by:

- experience of stigma;
- experience of separation and loss; and
- 'genealogical bewilderment'.

The experiences of many of those I interviewed bore this out. Several people referred to how easily identifiable Barnardo's children were by the drabness and uniformity of their clothing, but there was little attempt made at discretion in the system, as Ron explained, talking of the Barnardo's welfare officers:

> Every year they used to come round the schools to give us medicals and that. They used to come right out in front of the whole class and just say, 'are there any Barnardo's kids?' and put the scales on top of the door with everyone watching. 'Banana boys' the kids used to call you. And that wasn't very funny. It was all, 'where's your mum, where's your dad, you ain't got one', you know, and you had to carry that thing through life really.

Even those like Mary who were happily fostered were not immune to social stigma:

> Being a fostered child, the kids used to be so wicked, so did some of the grown-ups, called us 'guttermuck' and all this sort of thing. They'd heard you was in a home and that was it, not the reason why … it used to hurt us as kids.

The difference between Mary and Ron was that Mary had the protective support of a caring adult to help her through:

> We used to go home and tell mum, and she used to say, 'you can always hold your heads up high, you were chosen and they weren't'. She chose us and she loved us and that's why she had us.

It was the support of his foster parents which helped Pete cope with the stigma of racism in his childhood:

> I was out in a rural village where they hadn't even seen black kids or brown kids before, and people would stare and say 'why are you that colour and your mum's a different colour to you?' My mother would say to me, 'look, be smart, be yourself, don't give people cause to run you down, take no notice'. So I've gone through life like that, and its been great.

Pete was the only person I interviewed who was black or mixed race. The support of his foster parents, together with the presence of his sister to whom he was very close, made him feel comfortable and secure in his identity, even though he says:

> I don't feel as though I'm coloured or black. Most black people say, hey, going on about being called brother and so on – I'm a black person with a white inside, this is how I've been brought up. I don't need this black thing, don't need to have it. Most people say, at the end of the day, you've just got a good tan and that's it! (laughs). But that's how I feel.

Whilst some might consider that Pete had not come to terms with his ethnic identity, it was clear that Pete had resolved his own feelings about his identity, and for him it was not a problem; on the contrary his self-esteem was high.

During the period when all the interviewees were growing up, the stigma of illegitimacy was very great, and many Barnardo's children were affected by this:

> In those days, that was a slur. Specially when you went in the Navy, you were a bastard, they'd run you down to the lowest, so we never talked about it, hushed things up (Alf).

Such were the feelings of shame and the need for secrecy that neither Ron nor Alf told anybody about their past as they grew up – even Alf's wife and Ron's daughter were unaware of their Barnardo's connections until they decided to seek access to their records. This has dogged Ron throughout his life, causing him to lose friends and miss opportunities to advance his career:

I kept putting off moving to another job, because every time you moved you had to have a birth certificate and it was traumatic – didn't have a father's name on it, just the mother's, so everyone in the workplace knew ...

For Alf and Ron and others, their self-esteem was dented not only by the stigma of illegitimacy and being 'banana boys', but by their ignorance of their own backgrounds. This caused difficulties in accounting for themselves socially, leading to embarrassment, anger and bewilderment:

The most awkward part about being in the position we Barnardo's people were in is like, you'd join the forces or you was at school and they'd say, 'what's your father, is he British? Is your mother British?' And you'd just have to say, 'oh, British', but you don't know. Might have been Turkish, you'd never know, you just have to say yes. And you just don't know who you are, what you are, or anything about yourself really, only that you're a person and you've got a name and that's it (Fred).

The situation was most difficult for those in the 'rootless' group who had neither the knowledge of their original families (however painful or undesirable) to draw on, nor the cushioning effect of a substitute family whose identity they could at least to some degree adopt. I wondered how the interviewees had coped as children with their ignorance about their family backgrounds. Mary, Pete and Jim (the 'real families' group) and also Alf, all claimed never to have questioned their background as they grew up. Whether in a foster home or residential care, all were aware that they were not living with their birth parents, but:

I never thought about my background, I think you just accept it (Alf).

I was never really concerned about who my parents were, I was just under the assumption that they obviously didn't want me at the time, so why should I bother with them? I mean, I was quite happy as I was, I had foster brothers and sisters and we were just like one big happy family (Jim).

We understood that mum wasn't our ... biological mother, yes. But that didn't make any odds really, we'd got a mum, hadn't we? (Mary).

Mary explained that she had met her birth mother once –

When I was in hospital when I got run over, she had to come. But I don't remember her at all. She was probably just somebody, one of the people that were calling, it didn't mean anything to me. I never really gave it a thought.

Others had tried to work out what might have happened, but only Ann (who had known nothing about her origins) admitted, half-jokingly, to creating a fantasy family to fill the void, based on sharing the same surname as a major food manufacturer:

> I thought, maybe I'm a Batchelor's soup heiress and somebody'll show up and claim me one day!

Jean, who was removed from her abusive father after her mother's death, pointed out the problems in consolidating a sense of identity whilst growing up because of the lack of available mementos to preserve and reinforce memories throughout a childhood of changes and discontinuity. Explaining her longing to find photos and 'things other people take for granted', she said,

> I've got nothing until I left care and started having my own money and being able to accumulate around me a life.

The so-called 'rescued' group did not suffer the same problems of ignorance about their origins. However they probably experienced more than the others the sense of loss which came from either bereavement (Tom had lost his beloved father, and Jean her mother) or separation from family members (Bill was split up from his sister on admission to care) or from their familiar surroundings and culture. Tom, who was admitted to Barnardo's in late childhood after his father's death, illustrated how 'being torn away from somewhere I was safe, not knowing where we were going or what to expect', caused an acute crisis of identity for him:

> Suddenly it was as if someone had ripped the skin off my back, and pushed me out. I no longer existed as a person. I suddenly became a non-person.

The experience of loss in one form or other was common to all the interviewees, and many had suffered multiple losses. Combined with the stigma which so many had experienced in their childhood and the ignorance many felt about themselves and their origins, the result was often a sense of powerlessness and lack of control over their lives, and an erosion of self-confidence and self-esteem.

Conclusion

This then was the heritage of those Barnardo's children who came forward to seek access to their records. In order to make sense of what I was being told by those who had gone through the process of acquiring information about their past, I needed to understand this heritage. It was essential to listen to what they were telling me about their childhoods – their experiences and feelings about their families and about growing up in care, about what Barnardo's meant to them and how they felt about themselves as children – in order to grasp the significance to them of wanting to find out more about themselves. Only then could I hope to understand what impact their discoveries made upon them as adults, learning more about themselves in the middle and later years of their lives.

8 Motivation for Seeking Information

> I want my file – I want my life! (Ann).

The impact of gaining information about the past can only be properly understood by discovering *why* such information was being sought. The literature upon this subject is inconclusive but suggests that motivation for a search may be related to the quality of people's experiences of separation, loss and subsequent care in childhood. Having explored the experiences and feelings of my interviewees about their childhood, I sought to use this context to understand their motivation – expressed or otherwise – for seeking information. I also wanted to find out why people had made their enquiries at that particular time or stage in their lives. Other research studies had indicated that there were certain lifecycle triggers when people were more likely to want to search for their origins, in particular, marriage or divorce, having a baby, or the death of foster parents or adoptive parents. Walby and Simons (1990) had also noted that publicity (for example about changes in adoption law) could act as a trigger to seek information.

Triggers for Initiating a Search

I found little overt evidence from my interviewees of lifecycle triggers. The majority of my group were in fact grandparents, and for some at least, it is possible that the attempt to get information at this point was seen as a 'last chance' to resolve questions about their identity and origins which had been troubling them all their lives:

> I'd tried in my early years to find out, as one does, and I just couldn't get any information at all. I thought, I'll give it one more go, and if nothing happens, that's it (Ron, 74).

It was certainly apparent that publicity about the availability of information was a trigger for several who had not realised until then that such information – which they may have been seeking for a long time – was now available. For Ron, Ann and Bill it was the television documentary, *Barnardo's Children*, which acted as the trigger for their requests for information. The other interviewees had applied for their information before this documentary was shown, but Barnardo's own statistics reveal that the showing of this film was clearly a trigger for a great many people to request access to their records – over 4,000 in the month after the screening, compared to around 1,500 in the whole of the previous year.

Despite the common trigger though, the reasons and expectations behind the requests of Ron, Ann and Bill were very different. As already seen, Ron's life had been blighted by his ignorance about his origins and his lack of close attachments or family during childhood. Though not daring to raise his expectations too high, he had always harboured the hope that one day, someone would 'come looking for him', and his ultimate reason for seeing his records was the desire to discover and trace a family member.

Ann had similarly suffered from a complete lack of knowledge of her family background, but it was not the urge to rectify this which was specifically in her mind when she saw the television film. Though an intelligent and articulate woman, Ann had great difficulty in defining why she wanted to see her files. Seeing the documentary had a devastating impact on Ann – a tidal wave of memories flooded back, many of them unpleasant ones which she had no idea how to handle:

> I was absolutely shocked. I've always coped with everything, and suddenly it just brought back a whole lot of memories – things that I didn't even realise had happened, or I'd shut them away. It was instant, I was in floods of tears ...

Ann rang the telephone helpline constantly as the programme finished until she managed to get through to request access to her records:

> I wanted my file – I wanted my file NOW! I was absolutely obsessed, I was pacing up and down, raving like a lunatic. I don't know what I was expecting to find, I was more sort of angry, upset that they'd got all this information and I hadn't ... it was the fact that there was this building somewhere with the early part of my life tied up in it!

Ann's motivation and expectations for wanting her files were complex, and will be examined further below. Like Ron, the timing of her request was triggered not by any life-stage or event but by publicity showing that the information was actually available. Bill was also prompted to request access to his records by the BBC film but for somewhat different reasons. As one of the 'rescued' group, Bill had a fairly good knowledge of his family background. However through his life he had invested a great deal emotionally in creating a very positive image of Barnardo's as an organisation and as his 'family'. Negative comments about aspects of Barnardo's care made in the film had made him very angry; it was as though they constituted an attack on his parents and a threat to his very identity. Bill wanted his records in order to 'prove' to his own family of children and grandchildren that his memories of Barnardo's were not false, and to help them to understand what his childhood had really been like.

The final point to be noted when looking at what triggered people to seek information is that nearly half the interviewees said that the request for information was not actually their idea, but was initiated by someone else. In Fred and Alf's case, it was their children who had wanted to draw up a family tree and encouraged their fathers to contact Barnardo's:

> My daughter came over one day, and she said out of the blue – she was going on about her nephews and nieces, they've got two sets of grandparents and aunties and that – she said, Dad, we've got nobody, only on Mum's side. We've got no grandparents on your side. So I'd like to do a family tree, just to see what did happen (Alf).

In Jim's case it was his wife's idea, 'for the sake of the children', in order to complete their family history. Others were encouraged to search by friends or relatives who had had positive experiences of searching themselves. With so many of the group apparently dissociating themselves from having initiated a search for information, I wondered if there was an element of embarrassment or guilt around. Researchers such as Haimes and Timms (1985) for example had noticed adoptees' fear of being considered abnormal or obsessed in their search, whilst Walby and Simons (1990) had found some adoptees felt their actions were 'self-indulgent'.

I did not find any clear typological link between those who initiated the search themselves and those who were apparently prompted by others. What each person hoped for from their quest, and their degree of urgency to find out, varied greatly. These findings and their implications are looked at next.

Seeking One's Roots

Having listened to people reflecting on their childhoods and their feelings about themselves then, one might have expected that the 'rootless' group would have the strongest urge to seek information about their origins and to try to fill the 'genealogical void'. In some ways this was borne out, but I also realised that this group had often tried and failed to find information as they grew up, and at this latest approach to Barnardo's they lacked any confidence that this time would be different. Either they felt they might be too old for any significant information to have survived, or they feared Barnardo's would once again thwart any attempts to learn anything:

It could be just another disappointment (Ron).

I said to my daughter, this is going to be a waste of time, you won't find anything! (Alf).

June and Betty, both in their late 50s, were very specific in their reasons for approaching Barnardo's for information. They both hoped it would enable them to trace a relative. In Betty's case it was her mother, with whom she had had limited contact in her teens and with whom she had hopes of rekindling a relationship before it was too late. Betty wanted to know the reasons for her admission to Barnardo's as a baby. June wanted to find her brother and sister with whom she also had last had contact as a young woman. She had been trying to trace them for a long time through various means without success before realising that Barnardo's might hold crucial information to help her.

Ron, as previously described, knew nothing of his family background or reasons for going into care. He did not know who, if anyone, he wanted to find, but wanted in his mid seventies to have 'a last chance' to see if he could find anyone he could call his own. Although happily married with a grown up family, he felt he was 'a nobody' without any roots.

For each of these people there was a clear feeling that a vital part of themselves was missing and that they were not able, without the missing bits of the jigsaw, to fully work out who they were. This could also be said of the others in the 'rootless' group, Alf, Fred and Ann, but their expectations of ever remedying this situation were so low that until they were prompted into action by others, or by the television film, they had more or less resigned themselves to living with their ignorance.

Looking at the 'real families' group – Mary, Pete and Jim, they too shared an interest in knowing more about their origins, but their curiosity seemed considerably lower key. Mary was vehemently opposed to seeking out her abusive mother, but wanted information about her father, of whom she knew nothing. There seemed to be an element of wishful thinking in her motivation, a desire to somehow salvage her genetic inheritance by discovering that she had one 'good' parent to compensate for the 'bad' one she already knew about. However Mary frequently made comments to me such as, 'I'm not particularly bothered about it though, I'm quite happy as I am'.

Pete used almost identical phrases when asked what led him to seek information about his background. He had wondered whether his birth parents were still alive, but repeatedly stressed that this was 'just curiosity'. He said he would not have been particularly interested in meeting them even if it was possible, as he had had such a good upbringing with his substitute family and needed nothing more. He was still in close touch with his elderly foster mother, and clearly felt a strong loyalty towards her, though she had not stood in the way of his search for further information.

In Jim's case, he had acquiesced to his wife's urging to seek information about his origins, on the grounds that their children might one day want to know their roots. Fifty years after his admission to care he did not expect to find out any information of significance, and again, claimed to have very little concern on his own behalf, but acknowledged that this was a matter which might be important to his children:

> I was never really concerned about who my parents were, I mean, I was quite happy as I was. And I really didn't think I'd get any results, 50 years, it's a long while. But my wife said, why don't you try and find out, it'd be nice for the boys to know who, perhaps, my mother and father and gran and whoever were, or where I came from …

The search for roots, either on one's own behalf or for one's children, therefore figured largely in people's motivation for seeking information. For some, a little more knowledge was all they wanted, while for others, there were hopes of actually finding a relative. Some, such as Tom, knew most of their background, but sought confirmation of half-known facts and rumours. Others such as Ron started from a base of complete ignorance of their genealogy. It should also be mentioned that some sought genealogical information in order to get a medical history – Fred for example, whose daughter needed information about a rare condition afflicting her son which might be hereditary.

However the need to fill the genealogical void, significant though this was, was not the only motive for seeking information from Barnardo's. Another distinct reason could be identified, which is examined below.

Making Sense of the Past

It could be argued that receiving information about one's origins was an integral part of 'making sense of the past'. But some of the people I spoke to were seeking more than just information – they wanted explanations, or help to enable them to understand not just what had happened in their lives but how and why. Learning about unknown parents may have been a part of this, but they also wished to know about their time in care – why certain decisions were made, who made them, why they were moved to particular homes or separated from siblings. Some of the time, answers were unlikely to be found in their records – why wasn't I given affection, why was I abused? Yet it was crucial to the person's sense of identity and self-esteem that these answers were sought, and some such as Ann and Jean were convinced that their records would hold the key to unravelling these mysteries. Jean explained:

> I was old enough to remember when we went into care, but I wanted to know the other side, all the shenanigans which must have gone on before we were taken into care. I know Barnardo's knew my sister had been abused [by father] but I don't know if – I don't think for one minute they thought that I was. But the big question I wanted answered was whether my mother knew. And if she knew, why didn't she do anything?

Jean thought she had learned to cope with the legacy of childhood traumas, and indeed, could take pride in her marriage and family and professional career. However she had always battled against weight problems, and it was when she embarked on 'yet another weight loss programme' that it was suggested to her that her problems could have a psychological origin. This prompted her to seek answers to the questions about her past that had troubled her for a long time.

There were similarities in the backgrounds of Jean and Ann, having both suffered horrific abuse during their childhood. But whereas Ann – despite intense desperation to see her file once she realised it was accessible – could not define what she hoped to find from it, Jean had very specific hopes:

I wanted nitty-gritty, I wanted photos and bills and all the minutiae that made it real. I wanted my reports and I wanted to see my handwriting ... it's daft the things you actually do want, things other people take for granted ... I can't remember what my mother looks like, and I'd love a photo. I would also love photos of me when I was younger ... I've got nothing.

Jean summed up her feelings in the same words as did Ann:

I want my file – I want my life!

This declaration seemed to encapsulate the idea that knowledge about the past comprises a vital element in achieving a sense of completeness, of knowing who one is. Both Jean and Ann appeared to be well-adjusted personalities, in control of their lives, yet both were aware of elements beyond their control. Whilst for Jean it was her weight, Ann confessed:

I don't think I'd call myself totally normal. I'm a very insecure person, that's why I've got to have lots of material goods , you know, four TVs, three videos and so on ... always got to work to get this and get that. I'm proving myself or something.

It should be noted however, that both women felt proud of their achievements as parents, and included in their reasons for wanting to see their records their wish to give their children an awareness of their roots which they themselves had lacked:

I'd like him to know his roots, to have, not necessarily contact with anybody, just to know he's got a bit of family for his sake and the next generation (Ann).

To summarise, people expressed a variety of reasons for wanting to see their records. Some wanted general information to help them cope with either total ignorance of their origins or to fill in gaps in their partial knowledge. Some wanted this for the specific purpose of tracing a relative. Of those seeking this type of information some wanted it to build up their own sense of identity whilst others expressed a wish to give their offspring a heritage. For some it was more important to find out about their time in care or to seek an understanding of experiences from the past in order to integrate this into their present self-concept. The intensity of people's curiosity varied greatly, with those who had the least satisfactory experiences in childhood tending to express the strongest 'need to know'. For these Barnardo's children, it seemed most often to be the realisation that long-withheld information might now be available, rather than any particular life-event or stage of life, which triggered their requests. Whatever people's expressed motives or expectations, the chance to see their records seemed to be closely bound up with a search for identity. Only an understanding of their past would enable them to make sense of who they were now, and to help them feel complete.

9 The Impact of Receiving Information

The review of literature indicated that knowledge about one's origins is closely linked with the formation of identity and self-concept (McWhinnie, 1967; Triseliotis, 1973; Haimes and Timms, 1985; Walby and Simons, 1990; Brodzinsky et al., 1992). My study of people who sought such knowledge found that, despite a great diversity in their experiences, their lives were often overshadowed by loss, ignorance, a sense of powerlessness and a feeling of incompleteness. In varying degrees, they hoped that the information contained in their records would help them to make sense of their past and complete the jigsaw of who they really were.

The outcome of the quest for information was very different for each person, and its impact upon them was strongly linked to their past experiences and their hopes and expectations. This chapter tells some of their stories and explores the themes and thoughts which arose from them.

The Process of Getting Information

> They told me I'd have to wait a year, minimum, to see my file. So I went and got myself a solicitor and sent them a solicitor's letter. I was so screwed up, I mean really badly screwed up. I wanted my file *now*! You know, no amount of 'we've got a waiting list' – I didn't care! Sounds dreadful, but it's not the same person as after I'd seen that programme. Even the thought of a week was too long. Pretty different now – I've read it.

Ann was one of the 4,000 enquirers who rang the helpline following the *Barnardo's Children* documentary in 1995. Fortunately for her sanity, Barnardo's responded sympathetically to Ann's extreme desperation and she was able to meet a social worker and see her file a few weeks later. She described her reactions:

> I started feeling better once I knew I was going to get it and I wasn't going to

wait for a year. Because that's what was bothering me, I thought, I can't live like this for a year, I'll end up in the nut-house. And it was quite – when I read it, I thought, my god, is that it! 'Cos, I was all prepared for a big traumatic experience, and it wasn't. I'd sort of gone through the worst before I got to the file.

Ann's overwhelming desperation to see her file, which she did not fully understand herself at the time, seemed to be the one tangible thing to focus on which might somehow hold the key to sorting out the past. Reading her information was a continuation of the process started off when she saw the television programme – a process of triggering memories and emotions from her past, which, once brought to the surface could then begin to be faced and 'worked through':

> A lot of what had happened, I unlocked by seeing that programme, things that I'd forgotten or blocked out or whatever – it had gone.

Furthermore, not only was some of the therapeutic process achieved before even reading her file, but Ann discovered that none of her worst memories – or very few of them – were actually on the file. Ann was therefore no wiser about some of the questions which had haunted her, for example concerning the mental state of her foster mother:

> I can remember being sat on her lap in the kitchen, and I can remember her rocking me and telling me we were all going to die, things like that. I was taken away from her when I was seven … but, to all intents and purposes she was OK, she was like Jekyll and Hyde. I can see how Barnardo's didn't realise what she was like, and I don't know what alerted them to the fact something weird was going on. I'd love to have known that.

Whilst it is perhaps not surprising that some memories – particularly of incidents of abuse whilst in care – are not reflected in people's records, it does raise questions about what impact it has on the reader of the records, when the files seem to record a different version of their lives from that which they recall. I wondered whether this might have the effect of reinforcing people's childhood sense that they or their problems were invisible, or were not considered important enough to record. Might it induce a sense of self-doubt, wondering if something really happened after all? Or would this cause feelings of anger that their cries for help had gone unheard, that clues had been unrecognised?

None of my interviewees expressed these sentiments overtly, and, like Ann above, seemed able to see why the records had such omissions – for example, abuse may have been unreported or deliberately concealed. However it is possible that others may have reacted differently. Jean was disappointed by her records for different reasons, but ones which also raise the question of 'whose truth' is contained in the files. Jean had her information before the policy of fully open access to files was implemented, and was very aware that she was only able to read what someone else judged to be significant or appropriate for her to see:

> I wanted my file so I could look at every single piece of information that everybody knew of. I wanted to know everything that everybody knew. I wanted, you know, scraps of paper that have got things scribbled on, bits that people might say, I wonder what I wrote that for and screw it up and throw it out, I wanted to be able to rifle through a file for myself, I didn't really want this nice sanitised thing that had been sorted and printed out. But I didn't get the opportunity because the social worker selected what she thought I wanted and brought a package here and went through it with me.

At the time Jean saw her records it was also not policy to allow people to retain file material other than a limited number of basic documents, and Jean also found this frustrating:

> I wanted to actually have my bits and bobs so I could sit and ponder and look and think ... but you had to have somebody sitting at the table with you ... it smacks of them being defensive and not wanting you to see – not because of what you might find out about yourself, but what I might have found out about them!

It was precisely to address issues like this that Barnardo's did introduce their Open Access policy shortly afterwards.

There was another sense in which Jean was somewhat disturbed by what she found in her records. Although keen to learn about herself as a child, she was 'a trifle galled' to read 'judgemental' comments about herself which shattered her illusions about some of her carers:

> I thought, how can Aunty Pat have said that about me? She used to like me I thought! I saw her as *my* Aunty Pat, but she wasn't. She was somebody doing a job. When I read it, I thought, sneaky old devil! It was like somebody talking behind your back ...

Jean had been aware of her physical shortcomings as a child, and had tried extremely hard to compensate with academic success. Sadly though, her records seemed to reflect only her failings and not her efforts to overcome them:

> I knew I was podgy and spotty and had long greasy hair, and the only way I could redeem myself was to use my brain. So I proceeded to do it. And every year I came first in the class, which is why I wanted those reports. And I thought it would have said, 'Jean's working very hard at school', 'cos I was so desperate to prove something to them, that I wasn't just this horrible little child they were making me feel. And it didn't mention a thing, so I was a bit miffed at that. However much effort I tried to put into pleasing these people, they didn't actually see what I was 'sending out'.

Jean admitted that she had been warned by the social worker that some of the recording was very 'judgemental'. It seemed that comments of this kind about children could indeed have a powerful effect on the self-esteem of the adult reader. It was not inevitably a negative impact however; Ron was an example of someone whose files recorded very positive comments about him as a child. Ron seemed almost literally to puff his chest out as he read out phrases such as 'is well-mannered and intelligent' from his fostering reports. One can only speculate upon the effect it might have had on Ron's self-confidence had he received these praises during his childhood.

People's feelings about the social worker who shared their records with them were, apart from Jean's frustrations, unanimously positive, and almost all cited a positive value in their presence:

> He was a really nice bloke, which really helped when I was so uptight (Ann).

> She was pretty good really, put it over nicely and explained things. She was sorry she couldn't tell me more (Mary).

Even where the social worker had to impart painful news, or apologise for a dearth of information in some cases, there was rarely a hint of dissatisfaction with the bearer of the news. On the contrary, the overwhelming impression received was of gratitude and appreciation that someone had at last unlocked the secrets of the past, and had taken trouble to do this in a sensitive manner:

> He's got all the time in the world when he's talking to you, doesn't rush you, he's such a smashing chap (Bill).

Bill was the only person other than Jean who mentioned the 'hell of a long waiting list' for information as an issue. However, while this is undoubtedly a source of great frustration for many who are currently waiting to be seen, its low profile in this study is likely to be because some interviewees had been seen before the 1995 post-documentary rush, whilst others had been given priority on the waiting list. This may have been, like Ron and Alf, because of their age or health, or, like Ann, because of alleged abuse in care.

Although the evidence in this area was limited, it seemed that factors such as the way in which the request for information was dealt with, and the way the information was presented and shared with the enquirer all had a bearing on the impact of the information itself upon the enquirer. Records however did not always hold all the answers to everyone's questions, or necessarily reflect the memories or understanding of their subject; enquirers found that there could be more than one version of 'history'.

The Assimilation of New Knowledge from the Records

> We said, we've got a father! That made so much difference to us, knowing that, and as soon as that was mentioned, I was a different person. I feel as though something's been lifted off me! (Alf).

When Alf's daughter started seeking her father's roots, Alf had been very pessimistic about finding out anything. Although he and his sister had grown up together in Barnardo's they had never discussed their family background, even between themselves, because of their sense of shame about their presumed illegitimacy. None of Alf's family, let alone his friends, knew he had been a Barnardo's boy. The shattering discovery that he was not in fact illegitimate after all enabled Alf to really 'take the lid off' his past:

> My sister was a bridesmaid for me and the wife, she's godmother to our children, so we're always in contact with each other, but we've never spoken about our childhood. Until recently. Now we're phoning up and talking to each other all the time about it, and tonight I'm going to my local, and I'll probably talk to them about it all too and, you know, I'm not ashamed of it. I'm just as good as anybody else – I've got a family!

Alf made more discoveries, too. Through his daughter's efforts with various authorities, he discovered that he also had two brothers he had known nothing about. This produced powerful but conflicting emotions:

As soon as we found this out, we wrote to Barnardo's and asked them to explain to us why I wasn't told I'd got a brother. Well, the social worker came down with all these papers – she'd got my grandfather on there, mother's parents, everything. Brothers, sisters, there was such a load of it, and all these years we'd never known any of it! I didn't know whether to cry, or if I was angry. My daughter was crying, I was so – I *was* angry! I accepted the father bit, I was thrilled to bits with that, but when they said I'd got a brother then I was angry to think that I hadn't been told about it.

Alf had a great deal to assimilate. On the one hand, he was readjusting his self-image from the shame of his supposed illegitimacy and, by association, from the stigma of being a Barnardo's boy, to a new persona that he could be proud of and could now be open about socially. On the other hand, he needed to assimilate the idea that Barnardo's (who had claimed him as part of their family) had withheld vital information from him about his birth family. Thus he had been denied the chance to know his family as a child and as an adult, and to grow up with any sense of identity and belonging. Alf found his roots, but faced the task of reconstructing his image both of who he was and where he came from. He then felt able to present his new identity to his family and the outside world.

Like Alf, Jim had expected very little to come out of his search for his roots, and it was, also like Alf, his family who persuaded him to make enquiries. Unlike Alf, Jim felt his foster family had provided him with all the family life he needed, and he had felt little curiosity about his background. However a remarkable example of 'synchronicity' caused Jim, too, to have to assimilate facts about his origins which he had never anticipated:

> I wrote a letter to Dr Barnardo's – the first time that I'd thought about or decided to do this in 50 years. At the very same time, it's unbelievable, my sister – who I didn't know about then – was writing to different people to let them know her mother – *our* mother! – had died.

In short, the sister discovered by chance that she was related to Jim – a sibling relationship which neither had ever suspected existed. Within the same month, Jim saw his Barnardo's records and confirmed that this was definitely his younger sister, another 'secret', born after Jim's admission to Barnardo's, but this time kept by the mother. Issues around Jim's 'reunion' with his sister are explored later; but for both of them there followed, as in Alf's case, a long process of assimilating this discovery into their sense of identity, and of re-constructing their view of the past to accommodate this new information about their family. It challenged their sense of who they were and presented prospects of new family relationships. The clock could never be turned back again.

Both Alf and Jim were surprised and pleased with their discoveries, but whereas Alf, with little previous experience of a family to call his own, said he felt like a 'different person', Jim, who regarded his foster mother as his 'real' mother, reflected:

> To be honest, at the end of the day, the whole of this outcome, the person I feel most pleased for is Pauline [his sister]. Not for me, for Pauline. She had nothing. I just got another Christmas card at the end of the day!

Alf and his daughter used their new information to track down the burial place of his mother and had a headstone erected. Jim's sister wanted him to go to the crematorium where their mother was buried, but Jim was very reluctant:

> When my sister talks about mother, my mind reverts straight away to my foster mother. 'Cos that's the only mother I knew. I know she felt hurt, but when Pauline mentioned mother, it didn't mean anything to me. I'd never seen her – my mind can't communicate with her at all.

While Jim expresses some warmth towards his new-found sister, he appears to place little value on the blood tie itself. Although his sister grew up with their birth mother, this fact counts for little in his view ('she had nothing') against the relative hardships of her childhood compared with the close relationships with foster siblings, affection and security which he himself enjoyed as a child. This attitude seemed to be shared by all three of those whom I classified as belonging to 'real families' (Jim, Pete and Mary), and did not appear to be significantly changed by the acquisition of additional information about their families of origin. Furthermore, all three were anxious to stress that knowing more about their background had not changed their feelings about themselves:

> It didn't make me feel any different. I think I had such a good upbringing from the start, I mean, Mum always told us, even though she wasn't our real Mum, that she loved us, and that means a lot to a child (Mary).

Pete was pleased to get more details about his birth parents, especially their names and whereabouts. He explained that, had it seemed feasible to actually trace or contact either of his birth parents, then he would probably have felt tempted to do this 'just out of curiosity', and this might then have led to more far-reaching consequences for him emotionally. But as it turned out ...

> It seems that my father's not contactable, I mean, they don't know him from Adam actually. But as far as I'm concerned, that's probably better, 'cos if I knew he was living here in England, and if I knew they [mother and father] were both living together, then I would think, well I really would like to go and see them. But knowing he's gone back abroad and she's living with her own husband now, that's fine with me. I'm happy with that. I now know who my mother is, where I was born, what the circumstances are, etc. I really didn't want to go into it any further. And I can tell you that my real mother would never take the place of my foster mother. Never.

Even if some of those I interviewed felt that their new knowledge about their origins had little impact on their sense of themselves, most had, to some extent, had to assimilate new facts into their previously held assumptions about their background. Several who had not known why they had gone into care had made the assumption that they were unwanted or rejected by their birth parents. This happened to include all the 'real families' group, but was less prevalent amongst the others. When the facts challenged this assumption in some cases (for example, the mother who felt she had no choice in the social context of the times but to give up her illegitimate child, but who did so with great reluctance), then readjustments had to be made to some long-held beliefs, and sometimes the person needed to renegotiate their image of their birth parents.

Confusion occurred sometimes when new pieces of information did not tally with memories. Fred, for example, remembered going to a funeral which he thought had been that of his birth mother, but now realises it was his adoptive mother's. Alf had been convinced he had gone to his foster carers at the age of five, and was shocked to discover he had been seven, and has no memory of his two 'missing' years. On the other hand, the process of 'filling in' blanks from the past also had the effect of triggering long buried memories. In trying to understand the sequence of events in his childhood, Fred suddenly recalled a vivid memory of being taken to a Barnardo's Home for convalescence after an operation:

> They took me back in this ambulance, and there's the driver, and this woman in the back. They drew up two miles up the road and she got out and sat with him, and left me alone, and that was dark ... they just wanted to be together in that ambulance and they left me alone ...

Fred's memory seemed like a metaphor for his childhood feelings of fear and isolation and powerlessness. It also seemed to illustrate the process of incorporating new information with retrieved memories in order to make sense of the past.

The Impact of Photographs

Acquiring a photograph of oneself or a relative made a huge impact on each person who was fortunate enough to find this as part of their 'package of information' from Barnardo's. The organisation photographed most children on admission to care and again at school leaving age, but such photographs were not routinely given to the children themselves but kept in the archives. Many adults grew up having never seen or owned a single photograph of themselves as children. This had perhaps contributed to some people's struggles to gain a sense of identity or self-worth. Even Ann, who in her early 40s was one of the younger people I interviewed, had never seen a photograph of herself as a child before until she was given some at her file-viewing:

> I was so happy, because I could put them up next to my daughter's photos … we're almost identical, it's really funny. She cried, my daughter did, 'cos there I am, with a big number across my chest! She said 'you look like a little convict!'. It really upset her, but I was really pleased because I'd never seen a photo of myself. It was nice to have, never seen anything like it.

It was clearly important to Ann to see a physical resemblance to her daughter, which seemed to lend a feeling of 'connectedness' which had been so lacking in her life. Others also placed a high value on being able to see photographs of birth relatives even if – or especially if – they could not meet them in person. The seeking of physical likeness to a blood relative seemed to be an important part of establishing one's identity, as illustrated for example by Fred, who acquired a photograph of his mother whom he had no recollection of ever meeting:

> That was really something that you've seen who your mother is, that was something to know what she looked like because, I know a lot of children, if their parents are dead, they don't remember what their parents looked like but at least they usually have a photo. I hadn't even got that.

Mary also saw a photograph of the mother she could not remember, but found it distressing to discover a physical resemblance between herself and her mother when in all other respects she had wished to dissociate herself from any ties with the person who had been cruel to her:

> I do look like her [mother]. I felt upset about that. I was very disappointed – I didn't want to look like her. I wish I hadn't found out now. I know my ways aren't like hers anyway.

For Mary, the photograph had the effect of reminding her of the blood tie which she wanted to believe held no importance compared to the bond she felt with the foster mother who had loved and cared for her during her childhood.

Coping with Powerful Emotions

Whatever the nature of the information which people uncovered, it almost always generated powerful emotions in them, often taking them by surprise with their force. The exceptions to this were the 'real families' group, who tended to play down the impact of learning about their family background because of the relative value placed by them upon their *substitute* families. They often used expressions such as 'I was just curious' or 'I'm not that bothered' to indicate the lack of significance they attached to the process of finding out about their origins. I did wonder however whether there were sometimes elements of denial in their estimates of the impact upon them of learning about their birth families, perhaps from strong feelings of loyalty towards their substitute families.

The strength of emotion tended to be greatest amongst those who had known least about their origins and who were seeking to fill gaps in their lives left by childhoods which had provided little in the way of attachments or a sense of belonging. Alf illustrated this, describing the impact of discovering, firstly, that he was not illegitimate, and secondly, that he had had brothers he had not known about:

> This has been very, very moving. My daughter, she's had tears and tears and tears. When she cries, I have tears come … What makes it worse – I think it will always be like this – is when you see any programmes on TV where there's reunions or anything, they bring people on and they haven't seen each other for years and they're hugging each other – I'll sit there, and the tears they roll then, they do.

Many different emotions are engendered, from a feeling of catharsis and liberation such as Ann experienced after her initial turmoil, to the pain and anger of discovering too late that one had relatives one had not known about but who were now, as in the case of Alf's brothers, dead. Others like Fred had to cope with difficult information from the past which shocked them and brought into question whether they regretted having learned the information.

On reading his records, Fred learned that he was born of an incestuous relationship between his mother and her father. He was then adopted in some haste to try to avoid a scandal, although his adoptive mother died when he was only four years old, precipitating his admission to Barnardo's. These facts were obviously a source of considerable embarrassment to Fred, and whilst admitting they were 'a bit of a shock', he tries to brush aside the emotional impact upon him, preferring, not unnaturally, to concentrate on subsequent developments:

> ... that's the piece that really shocks you in the beginning, but after that, once you got over the initial shock and read on, you forgot the initial bit, then the other part really fits in, you know, you understand things more.

On a happier note, Fred was thrilled to discover that he had a large number of half-siblings, some from his grandfather's marriage and some from his mother's later marriage. Although his main goal had been to find out about his origins, it was a very welcome 'bonus' to also find he had relatives who could possibly even be traced. The positive things which came out of Fred's quest for information about his past seemed to have far outweighed the painful aspects of his discovery. He said he had no regrets about embarking on his 'journey', and would not hesitate to recommend others to do likewise. He summed this up by saying:

> ... that was a shock, but I'd rather I knew. At least you don't have to wonder about it any more.

This sentiment was echoed by others also; however painful the contents of their information, most people felt that they would rather know than remain in ignorance. The exception to this was 59 year old Betty.

Betty had approached Barnardo's for information with a view to trying to trace her mother. She had memories of occasional visits from her mother whilst she was in a children's home, which were not terribly happy memories. However she hoped that by finding out more about her she would understand her mother better and could perhaps have an adult relationship with her to make up for what she had not had as a child. Unfortunately when Betty read her records she found her mother had been violent and abusive towards her as a young child, and was extremely upset by this. It severely affected Betty's already poor health, and she needed counselling and medical help. She says she 'hates and despises' her mother, yet still cannot get her out of her mind, and keeps wondering if she is still alive. Betty found the counselling helpful, but still does not like talking about her mother and now wishes she had not read her records.

There was a happier outcome for Tom, despite also having to come to terms with overpowering emotions on initially reading his file. Tom had come into Barnardo's late in his childhood after the death of his much-loved father, and so had a basic understanding of the reasons for his admission and his family background. He hoped his records would fill in a few gaps and confirm or deny for him some facts he was unsure of. He was completely unprepared for the strength of emotion which enveloped him on reading his file:

> As I was reading through the notes, tears started running down my face. I knew my dad died, I knew what he died of, I saw him before he died and I knew he wasn't coming back, but what I couldn't get over – was that suddenly all that information about my mother and her illness, and the fact that she had us back when she wasn't fit to look after us – suddenly, all that information brought my dad back to life. And I was suddenly reunited with the grief that I thought I'd actually got nailed down. All that old grief and pain suddenly welled up.

Tom decided to have counselling at this time, and found this very helpful:

> What came out of that was that I'd never actually let my dad go. All those memories that came flooding back, they opened up a wound I thought I'd sealed for ever. And when I came for that Barnardo's information, it burst like a boil. But now my father is at peace. And I'm at peace with him. I can think of him with sadness but it doesn't bug me any more, it's laid him to rest.

Looking at how Tom and the others coped – or didn't cope – with the painful or difficult aspects of learning about themselves and their backgrounds, I tried to discover what strategies they used to help them. I also wondered how it was that people who had described so many losses and so much grief in their early lives had survived these and now appeared – in the majority of instances – to lead stable, settled and satisfying adult lives. Those in the 'real families' group made it clear that they felt that the love and stability of their foster families had enabled them to face the future with confidence, but how had those with less satisfactory experiences survived?

Applying the concepts of Fonagy et al. (1994) that there are a number of protective factors which can contribute to resilience, I looked for these factors in my interviewees. I certainly found considerable evidence of individual qualities such as intelligence, a sense of humour, the ability to organise one's thinking and reflect on issues, and a high degree of individual autonomy amongst many of those who might have been expected from their life stories to have had difficulty in coping in later life. Social factors identified by Fonagy such as high levels of family support, and religious belief were also much in evidence. Most of the interviewees had supportive partners (in nine out of the 12 cases these were the people they had married shortly after leaving care), and a similar number spoke warmly of close relationships with grown up children. All Barnardo's children were brought up with a high degree of religious input in their childhoods, and whilst this had put some off religion for life, others gained considerable spiritual strength or comfort from these early foundations.

I felt that these 'protective qualities' had indeed helped many people to cope, both with their childhood experiences and later in their lives, to deal with the emotional and often painful impact of learning about their origins. Other factors which people identified as protective included, in Pete's case, growing up with his twin sister:

> We were together ... we lived in our own little shells, so there wasn't a problem.

Bill found strength from the ethos and the staff of his residential home, Goldings, which he felt gave him skills, opportunities and a sense of pride in being a Barnardo's boy. Ann, who perhaps had the most difficult childhood of all the group, felt her 'saving grace' was the experience of going into a 'normal' family during her last year before leaving care, with a 'smashing' foster mother – 'even for a year, that really helped me'. Jean on the other hand attributed her self-esteem and confidence in herself as a parent to the influence of her beloved mother, who had died before Jean came into care:

> She was always very caring ... I'm sure I would have got that from her.

Jean also felt that attitude had much to do with how you coped with adversity, and these factors seemed to have enabled her to survive the sexual abuse she suffered in her early childhood:

You have to laugh at these things or you go through life with a huge chip on your shoulder.

Apart from protective factors, it was possible to identify different strategies which people used to cope with difficult or distressing information. These ranged from denial of any hurt ('that hasn't bothered me, I've got hardened to it'), to a rather fatalistic attitude of resigned acceptance ('It wasn't meant to be', or 'it's just bad luck isn't it'). Some were determined to look on the bright side, such as when Jim discovered that his birth mother had lived very close to him but he had never known her and now it was too late:

> That was rather sad to think we might have walked past her a hundred times and not realised. But then, I think things have worked out well really, because she was 80-odd and not a well person towards the end, and if I'd suddenly turned up, the shock would have killed her, wouldn't it?

Most people, having had time to reflect since getting their information, were able to rationalise and tried hard to understand and justify the actions of their birth families, however unpalatable the facts may have been. The greater the emotional investment in the birth family, the more people were prepared to empathise with or excuse their past failings. June for example talked about her mother who had both neglected and repeatedly rejected her:

> Apparently while she was married, she was fine. It wasn't until my father died, I think it just threw her and she went to pieces. Then she started going out with other men, and shoplifting, thieving, that sort of thing. She just lost interest in the children I suppose ...

Everyone, then, found different ways of coping with the range of emotions generated by reading their files. Clearly though, the impact of this experience was not felt in isolation by the person reading their information. It had reverberations upon those closest to them, and this was another area I sought to investigate.

Reverberations and Reunions

I was curious as to the impact on the interviewees' immediate families (partners and children) of this gaining of information about the past, with all the powerful emotions which this aroused in each person. It seemed as though the interviewees themselves had often been taken by surprise at the feelings which reading their records had brought up, and I wondered whether their families found this difficult to cope with, or whether perhaps the interest in their past had left families feeling at all excluded or neglected.

The finding that many people started their search with the explicit encouragement of friends or family may help to explain the very supportive attitudes which seemed to be held by people's partners and children generally. In Alf's case, for example, his daughter had been actively involved with him in seeking out information, and the shared 'journey' appeared to have brought them closer together:

> We've become really close, me and my daughter, she thinks the world of her dad! She's a lovely girl.

Sometimes though, it has also been a painful experience for the relatives, who may be less inhibited about expressing their feelings, or who may feel distress on behalf of their parent or partner for what he or she has to cope with. This was illustrated particularly by Ann and her daughter. Not only did the daughter suffer during her mother's period of 'hell' after seeing the BBC documentaries – 'I was driving my daughter mad, poor thing, she was frightened to open her mouth'- but her daughter was 'absolutely horrified' to discover what her mother had been through as a child. Moreover, it is her daughter's reactions to this information which bring home the horror of it all to Ann herself:

> She was more upset and angry than I was at one point. I mean, yes, we were made to get up and scrub and wax the floor, people who wet the beds were plunged into baths of cold water and things like that, but I'd known all this and she hadn't. I wasn't aware that we'd been badly treated until that brought it home to me. Because I've never had a family, you don't know any differently.

Ann added however that she felt the experience of reading her files had 'given her [her daughter] a better understanding of why I'm like I am'. Like Alf and his daughter, I got a strong impression that going through everything together had strengthened the bond between them.

There is a considerable body of research and literature about reunions between separated relatives (usually concerning parents who are reunited with a child given up for adoption), and I did not set out to explore this specific topic in depth, aiming to focus primarily on the impact of the *information* about their origins which people gained. Nevertheless, for several of the people

I interviewed, the tracing of a birth relative was an important aspect of their motivation for wanting access to their files. For others, a reunion was an unexpected outcome of finding out more about their birth families. It seemed as though, if the wish to find relatives was not already something of an obsession (as it was with June for example), the discovery of new information often led to a thirst for even more. I heard people using phrases such as 'it bugged me, I thought, I've *got* to find out' (Tom), or 'I got a bit of a fixation' (Mary). In some instances, it was not until reading the files that the person realised for the first time that they actually *had* relatives who might be traceable. Alf knew that his parents could no longer be alive, but having discovered that he had brothers he had not previously been aware of, he was extremely keen to try and trace them. Fred also learned of his siblings for the first time from reading his files and immediately embarked on a search for them, with his social worker's help. Ron had always hoped he might have some family somewhere but had hardly dared raise his hopes of ever finding anyone. On finding out that he had a half-brother, he too had no hesitation in trying to find him. These three men, whom I had classified as belonging to the 'rootless' group, all had a high emotional investment in finding a blood relative to whom they could feel a sense of belonging – indeed, who could perhaps provide them with some 'roots'.

By the time of my meeting them, Alf, Fred and Ron had all made great progress in their searches, with the help of social workers and the Salvation Army Family Tracing Service. With enormous dedication to the task, and support from his family, Alf found out a great deal more information about his brothers, but sadly found that one had died a few years previously, and has so far been unable to find the other. He was delighted to meet people who had known his brothers, and to get photographs of them, and to hear glowing testimonials of their characters. I had a strong sense of the huge excitement involved in the discoveries, and the fact that others spoke well of Alf's brothers seemed to give Alf a boost to his own self-esteem. But there was also of course great sadness at the knowledge that the discovery, at least in one brother's case, had come a few years too late:

> I stood beside the grave, and my brother's lying in that grave, and I'm thinking, if only I'd done this five years earlier, he'd have still been alive. He was only 67 when he died, and he wasn't married. I could have had him here, living with me and my wife, but I don't even know what he looks like ... we had a spare bed, he could've come and stopped with us when he retired, or even just for holidays, that would have been beautiful. He could've still been alive, couldn't he, with us looking after him?

Alf's pleasure was mixed with sadness about what might have been had he started his search earlier, although on balance, he had no doubts that he was glad he embarked on the search:

> If anyone asked me if they should do the same, I'd say, oh *yes*! Do it straight away!

As mentioned earlier, Fred found out from his records that he, too, had some siblings he had not known existed. He took little time to decide to try and find them. With the help of the social worker, some of his half-siblings *were* traced, and to Fred's great surprise and joy, he found out that his mother, though very elderly, was still alive. This provoked a whole mixture of emotions and complications, as one side of the family were unaware of the other side's existence, and few had known of Fred's existence. There had been many agonising moments when decisions were taken about how much of the truth should be revealed and to whom, and what the reactions of his siblings and others might be to finding out about Fred. I asked Fred his reactions:

> Ooh, marvellous, 'cos to know you've got a family is something! But at the moment no-one'll tell me where my mother is. I have to send messages to mother through them [siblings], but I never get a reply what she's saying, they just say she's alright or whatever ... I've always wanted to know who my mother was, I've found my mother but now I can't meet her. I can't force them to let me see her or give me her address – that is frustrating!

Concerning those siblings who were traced, Fred had a mixed reaction. Some 'didn't want to know', one was abusive, but Fred is now getting to know others, who – after overcoming their initial shock – have accepted him as a brother, much to his delight. In fact Fred found to his amazement that 'they've accepted it better than I did really!'.

Fred was fortunate to have the full support of his wife through the ups and downs of these developments, and I saw no evidence of any negative impact upon her of Fred's journey of discovery. Being of a similar age to Alf, Fred did however share the same regrets about what might have been, had he had his information and found his family earlier:

> Too many years have gone by. My half-sister came and she said, how nice it would have been to grow up knowing each other when you were younger and not when you're older. You can't do the things which you could have done if it had been even 10 years ago, like I can't drive now like I used to ...

Fred still hopes that one day he may meet his mother, but is painfully aware that time is running out. Like Alf though, he had no doubts that the positive outcomes of his search had by far outweighed the rest, and was very glad that he had sought his information.

Perhaps the happiest outcome of all was Ron's. His half-brother was successfully traced, and after an exchange of letters, they had met for the first time four months prior to my meeting with him. Even when a relative is traced, there is of course no certainty that they will agree to have any contact, or that they will be happy to have been found. But in this case, not only Ron's brother but the whole of his large and very close-knit family embraced Ron (both literally and metaphorically) as a member of their family. Ron, a shy man under normal circumstances, was overwhelmed:

> They were all there to meet me when I went over – him and his wife and children, and their children – so from not having anyone, now there's 11 of them! To see them all there, making for me, took a bit of handling actually. And they all give you a hug, even the big fellow – over six foot he is! I'm just not used to this set-up – I hardly get one from the wife, never mind anyone else!

Ron showed me photographs of his new family, and his huge grin spoke volumes for his feelings. He was still finding it hard, though, to make the mental adjustment from being 'a bit of a lone wolf' to accepting his new identity as part of an extended family:

> It's unbelievable really. You feel as if you're walking on air. You can't take it in, even now. But I still feel – and everybody says it's silly to feel that way, but I do, you can't help it – I still feel like a bit of an intruder really. 'Cos obviously, your whole life you've been living as one person, not as a family thing …

Like Alf and Fred, Ron's only regret was that he'd 'lost a lot of years'. The excitement of discovering his 'lovely' family is marred only by thoughts about how much he has missed out on by not finding them earlier in his life. Ron talked about his happiness, and also explained that finding his family had made a big impact on another aspect of his life:

> I feel a lot more comfortable with myself. I mean, in the old days, you'd meet somebody and get on with them and then you'd find that they start talking about families and that, and you think, here we go again, so that friend's dropped, you know … But I was amazed how people took it [when they heard about finding his brother]. Now I'll tell anybody, like I told that lady in the post office about the brother I never knew I had!

Not only had finding his family made Ron feel more confident socially, it also affected the relationship with his daughter, whom he had never told about his Barnardo's background:

> Actually it was a bit hard for her as a child, 'cos I never said anything to her at all, but she obviously thought there was something a bit ... different, a bit dubious about my background, but she never asked. She thought, well, if he doesn't want to tell me ... But she's really thrilled about it all. In fact, when I mentioned that it was my brother's birthday the other day, she said, oh, I was going to get him a card anyway!

Ron and his wife talked to me about the likenesses and similarities between their family and the brother's family, and seemed to gain considerable pleasure from being able to place Ron in a genealogical context, to identify the genetic connections, and to be understand his origins.

Former Child Migrants

Although not forming a part of this study, particular mention should be made at this point of the special circumstances of those who emigrated as children to former colonies and Commonwealth countries whilst in the care of child care agencies such as Barnardo's. Child migration schemes were once a mainstream part of childcare practice, encouraged by the British government and the governments of the receiving countries, and undertaken by a variety of charities, church organisations and local authorities. Today, schemes where deprived children are shipped to another continent, cut off from former family and friends, seem inhuman. Historically however the prevailing ethos was one of 'rescue', removing children from both undesirable family situations and overcrowded children's homes to a fresh start in a healthier and more promising part of the world. It also held the more dubious possibility of populating the emptier parts of the British Empire with white English stock (Humphreys, 1994). A parallel may perhaps be drawn with current inter-country adoption practice which may be viewed with similar outrage by future generations.

Barnardo's sent 30,000 children to Canada between 1882 and 1939, and just under three thousand to Australia between 1883 and 1965. The vast majority of Barnardo's children who emigrated to Australia went between 1921 and 1939. Providing these former child migrants with information from their records and helping them to trace relatives in the UK has been a significant part of the workload of Barnardo's After Care service for many years. For many, the sense of loss and confusion arising from their separation from families and lack of family background information is greatly compounded by the separation from their country of origin. A need to resolve issues of ethnic and cultural identity increases their hunger for information. One former child migrant expressed it thus:

> Nearly everyone treasures his or her earliest childhood memories … but not every man or woman has access to such precious recollections. Some of us have grown up in limbo, as if we had landed on earth from outer space, always a stranger among strangers, unable to recall no matter how hard we try, where we came from or how we got here (Allan Moore, *Growing up with Barnardo's*).

The experience within After Care has been that such information also has tremendous impact upon the descendants of the migrants. Few of the Canadian migrants themselves still survive, but their families still feel a deep inherent sense of loss because of what their parents went through. Unlike Australia, Barnardo's has no office in Canada, and most enquiries and requests for information have to be dealt with by post. An annual visit to Canada by After Care staff provides former child migrants and their families with their only opportunity to talk personally about these issues. The Head of After Care described a recent visit:

> It was like arriving with bread in a place where there's been a food shortage. Queues of people desperate to be fed – but with facts not food. I have met 100 year olds, 90 year olds and people in their 70s – all once Barnardo's children – many of whom have gone through a lifetime never talking about their childhood because of shame and stigma. Nor have they known the true facts about their own lives. People are hungry for information about their origins. They have been starved for too many years (Bradford, 1998).

Letters received in After Care following this visit record the impact upon some former child migrants who subsequently received information from their records:

> The records and photographs arrived through the post on the day Florence [who emigrated to Canada with her sister in 1922] had to move into a nursing home – the joy those pictures and information brought to that 86 year old lady was beyond imagination. We spent the whole afternoon listening to Florence talk about her life. Thank you all so much, you are bringing so much joy, peace of mind and satisfaction to Barnardo's people and their descendants (friend of Florence).

The son of a former child migrant wrote explaining that learning the facts of his mother's early life – her father's struggle to look after a family of seven when his wife died; her admission to Barnardo's Village Home in Barkingside, England and her emigration to Canada in 1911 – was a painful process, but helped put previously unexplained things into place for him:

> I only found out after her death that my mother had been a Barnardo's girl. She never talked about the unpleasant, disappointing and sad times of her childhood but she became a very special lady and mother ...

Other former child migrants who gained access to their records were able for the first time to see letters and explanations given by their birth parents, concerning not only their admission to Barnardo's care but also what led to them being emigrated to the other side of the world. Like many adults who grew up in care, many had assumed that they were unloved and unwanted by their parents. For some at least the records provided evidence to the contrary. One such was 73 year old Stanley, whose records contained a letter from his mother to Barnardo's saying:

> I am willing for him to go to Australia as he will be well cared for there. I only wish I could have given him a home but it is impossible for me to do so now.

Even the smallest indications such as these that the child had once been the subject of some parental concern or affection appeared to have a dramatic impact upon the self-esteem and peace of mind of the adult recipient.

Reflections – An On-going Process

For the study I deliberately chose to interview people at least a year after they had read their records (see Methodology), and I encouraged people to reflect upon the impact they felt the experience had had on them and those close to them. I was interested to hear how their new knowledge had influenced their feelings about themselves, their birth families, their current partners and children, and towards Barnardo's, their 'corporate family'. As has been shown, experiences and feelings varied widely, depending on where metaphorically people were coming from and what they had hoped to achieve, and on the nature of the information they learned. One universal outcome however, was that no matter how much information was contained in the records, it never provided *all* the answers to people's questions. Although more of the 'jigsaw' might be completed than ever before, there were always areas on which one could only speculate. Some had felt impelled to make continuing investigations of their own, and some were still trying to trace relatives. But for everyone, there was an ongoing internal process of assimilating new information into their existing knowledge, re-evaluating the past and present in the light of new facts, and often retrieving buried memories from childhood which were triggered by reading their files.

Part of the reflective process often included reassessing their attitude towards Barnardo's. Some, such as Pete, Mary and Jim saw Barnardo's as the provider of good loving substitute families. Bill, Tom and Jean felt grateful to Barnardo's for rescuing them from unhappy family situations. By and large, their discoveries about their pre-Barnardo's origins served to confirm for them the feelings that they had been better off in care than if they had remained with their birth families. Some of their positive feelings were attributed to their foster parents, some to a specific residential establishment, whilst others expressed appreciation of Barnardo's itself.

Amongst the others I interviewed – who all fell into my 'rootless' category – attitudes towards Barnardo's after getting their information were more complex. Growing up as children with little knowledge of their families of origin and few if any family contacts, they had been actively encouraged to see Barnardo's as their family, and had been taught to be grateful to Barnardo's. However their experiences of care had not always been happy, and some seemed to have little to be grateful about. Several of them, particularly Ann and Alf, reflected that, as children, because they had never known anything different, they had accepted their lot and assumed that was what life was like.

As adults they had formed new relationships and had children of their own and had learned that family life could be different:

> I think all Barnardo's children appreciate family life when they get married and that. You've never had it. I mean, when you work it out, we never had a childhood, did we? (Alf).

When the likes of Alf, Ann, Fred, Ron, June and Betty read their files, and found that they had families whose identities Barnardo's had kept secret from them – siblings they had not known existed, or parents who they had been misled into believing were long dead – they felt very divided loyalties towards Barnardo's. Several openly expressed their anger about the information and opportunities which they had been denied. But anger was often tempered by genuine appreciation of the positive aspects of their childhood which they felt Barnardo's had provided, and by people's efforts to seek explanations for the policies and practices of the past:

> Judging by what I found out about my father – a bare-knuckle fighter, living in a gypsy caravan – I can see why they [Barnardo's] would have wanted to protect me from all that, though I don't think it was right that they told my family I'd died!

Ann summed up the overall impact upon herself of reading her files by saying 'it's given me a better understanding of myself, and why I am like I am'. In common with almost all the interviewees, she felt on balance pleased that she had undertaken her quest for information. Despite the mix of emotions their information engendered, the consensus seemed to be that their knowledge was a positive contribution to their 'sense of self'. With the exception of Betty, nobody regretted having seen their information, and all said they would have no hesitation in recommending others to do the same. The impact of the experience may have been very different for each person, but as Sanders and Sitterly (1981) wrote:

> The completed search is not the end, but is only the beginning. We cannot go back now. We are, without exception, different than when we naively began our journey to recapture the lost past. But we are more, never less, than when we began.

PART 3
THEMES AND THOUGHTS

10 Themes Arising from the Study

Part 3 is divided into two broad sections: firstly an analysis of the theoretical issues which emerged from both the literature survey and the reflections of the adults I interviewed about their experiences of receiving information about their origins. Secondly, some policy and practical implications of these findings are considered.

The Meaning and Significance of Roots

Central to this study has been the theme of roots. Whatever people's age and stage of life, and whatever relationships they may have developed during their lives, they demonstrated an interest – sometimes a preoccupation – with looking back to the past for their roots. All the people I studied had achieved at least a degree of fulfilment in their adult lives – many appeared to be happily married and took pride in their role as parents or grandparents, some had satisfying careers, others could point to creative talents such as poetry writing. Yet all had chosen, or been persuaded, to approach Barnardo's in order to explore their past. This was in spite of the knowledge that invariably separation and loss (and often multiple losses) formed part of the route map through their past. The decision to open 'Pandora's box' therefore involved a considerable risk – the risk of invoking pain, sadness, disappointment or anger. Yet all felt the potential gains of taking this step outweighed the risks of negative outcomes.

The expressed objectives of the participants in the study in asking to see their records were very varied and complex. While some were explicit that they wished to find information to enable them to trace relatives, others found it difficult to identify what they sought, or they attributed their reason for searching to the needs of someone else close to them. Triseliotis (1973) found that those whose early experiences were mainly unhappy had a stronger need both for information and to trace relatives. Those who had enjoyed a secure substitute family life showed curiosity rather than a hunger for information. This was largely borne out in my study. Those I called 'rootless' shared a strong desire to find biological links, whether explicitly hoping to actually meet a relative, or expressing a wish for knowledge about their genealogy and family background. No matter how apparently satisfactory their current relationships might be with their partners or children, they attached much importance to seeking their roots through blood ties.

'Roots' were also valued by the 'real families' group of people who had been largely brought up in long-term foster families. However, the meaning they attached to roots lay not in the biological connection but in the bonds created by stability, a sense of belonging and of being loved and wanted, and a sense of permanence. For these people their biological origins were a source of some curiosity and interest, but because they already felt 'rooted', their need to know was less intense, and they perceived less risk in uncovering the past.

The Need to Know

The need to know could be seen as a continuum from, at one end for example, Pete's shoulder-shrugging attitude of being 'just curious' but 'not really bothered' to, at the other extreme, Ann's intensity of pain and feelings of such urgent need that she even considered how she might break in and steal her records rather than join a waiting list. A definite link could be discerned between the level of intensity of the 'need to know' and the quality of care experienced in childhood.

The nature of *what* people wanted to know varied greatly. Sometimes this need seemed to operate at an unconscious level, so that Ann, for example, despite knowing she very much wanted her information, was unable to identify exactly what she wanted to know, beyond her words:

> I don't know what I wanted to find out, but it was just, there's this building somewhere with the early part of my life tied up in it.

Many seemed to sense that whatever was in their records, it represented a part of themselves, some element that had been missing or could not be properly understood without the missing pieces of the jigsaw. Throughout the interviews and in the literature certain metaphors kept recurring – references to 'keys' to the past, or information which would 'unlock' the doors. Ann talked about how the television documentary 'unlocked memories' which she had buried or blocked out; Ron spoke of at last 'turning the key in the lock', in reference to Barnardo's opening up access to their records, though his words too could perhaps be taken as a metaphor for some unconscious search for a key to something less tangible in his life.

All those I spoke to had had to live with uncertainty and ignorance about who they were and what had happened to them. Several expressed feelings of frustration and impotence at the wall of secrecy they had encountered when asking for information in the past. Where the need for information was felt very strongly, people not only needed to know for their own psychological integrity, but also reported difficulties in accounting for themselves to others. Walby and Simons' (1990) found similar feelings in their respondents and concluded:

> The majority of respondents had, because of the secrecy and evasiveness experienced, developed the attitude that adoption was shameful and abnormal.

Like Ron and Alf and others in my study, the process of gaining information about their origins enabled these respondents to overcome their previous embarrassment and reluctance to talk about their origins, almost akin, suggests Walby, to descriptions of homosexuals 'coming out' (1990, p. 87).

Making Sense of the Past

This theme was a central one in this study. People sought information about their past for a variety of reasons, but only by examining how the material was subsequently evaluated and assimilated by the recipients can the real impact of this experience be understood. Life span development theory (Sugarman, 1986) has drawn attention to the notion that development continues throughout the life-cycle, and suggests that people's assimilation of new information is not likely to be a once-and-for-all event taking place at a particular moment in time or stage of life. Rather, there is a dynamic, lifelong process of reflection and review, so that each person is shaped by a whole range of events, relationships, achievements, losses and so on, which have different meanings at different points in their lives. However the situation in which the adults interviewed found themselves is, in developmental terms, far from the norm as conjured up by Kornitzer (1971), whereby:

> Background knowledge of one's family is like babyfood – it is literally fed to a person as part of the normal nourishment that builds up his (or her) mental and emotional structure ...

The adults in the study were already distinguished from the majority of the adult population by virtue of having been severed from their birth families in early childhood, but even within that grouping were highly unusual in the degree of ignorance of their family background which most had experienced right up to their mid- or later years of life. Once they had gained access to their records, despite disappointment for some that not *all* their questions had been answered, most had a considerable amount of new information to assimilate. This seemed to be a complex process, as a new fact might trigger other memories, which then needed to be re-evaluated in the light of the newly acquired information. Recounting and explaining information to others was another part of the process of evaluation. Ann illustrated how her daughter's reaction to revelations about abusive experiences made her realise for the first time that these experiences had indeed been abusive. This in turn gave rise to new and painful emotions in Ann as long-suppressed memories and flashbacks to her childhood emerged, and she struggled to make sense of what she had been through from an adult perspective.

As Haimes and Timms (1985, p. 71) found, a distinction could be drawn between those on the one hand who felt able to incorporate what they learned into their existing selves (such as Jim, whose reunion with a sister, for example, caused minimal disruption or change to his feelings about himself), and those on the other hand who seemed to need to reconstruct a new self – a 'pre-' and 'post-information' image of themselves.

When Alf discovered in his late 60s that he 'had a father', after going through all his childhood and middle years believing that he was illegitimate, and feeling so stigmatised by this that he kept the fact of his Barnardo's past a secret from even close friends and family, he said,

> That made so much difference knowing that! I'm a different person ... I'm just as good as anybody else!

For those like Alf, the knowledge that the stigma of illegitimacy had been removed produced very powerful emotions of elation, pride, relief, perhaps of liberation. The impact on Alf's self-image and self-esteem seemed somehow to be more profound than might have been expected from this particular piece of knowledge, even allowing for a generational perspective on attitudes towards illegitimacy and morality. It seemed to lend new meaning to 'being a legitimate person'. This concept was reinforced by memories of others who contacted Barnardo's After Care Section, such as Doris. Though married with children and grandchildren and a home of her own, she described herself as 'a nobody', because she was illegitimate and had no knowledge of any member of her birth family. To feel oneself a 'legitimate person' would seem to imply the need to feel 'rooted', and that this concept is valued – by those who have felt a lack of rootedness – more highly than almost any other.

Whether information is incorporated into existing self-image or used to reconstruct a new self, it follows that it is not just the past which is re-evaluated. The on-going process of assimilation enabled people to 'make sense of' where they had come from, but also affected both their present and their future selves. To varying degrees people were changed by their knowledge – as were those close to them – and in either a positive or a negative sense, their future would be different.

Intensity of Emotion

A very striking feature of these interviews was the intensity of emotions described by the participants, in relation to both their past and present lives. This perhaps in part underlines just how extraordinary were their situations and experiences, although they had not been knowingly selected on the basis of being extreme examples of a phenomenon. Nevertheless between them they had experienced extremes of loss, rejection, fear and pain on the one hand, but also (for example on Ron's first meeting with his brother or Alf's discovery that he had a legal father) enormous pleasure and joy which were often described as 'overwhelming'. Because of the intensely painful nature of some of the childhood experiences – feeling lonely and unloved in residential or foster homes, physical or sexual abuse by a parent or carer, the death of a much-loved parent, repeated rejections by family – the people I saw had had to develop their own strategies to deal with this amount of pain in order to preserve their mental health and survive. (All those in this study were very much 'survivors'; but experience of other Barnardo's After Care clients shows that many still struggle with depression, addiction, suicidal feelings, social isolation and so on.)

Some people seemed to have used denial as a means of dealing with their hurt ('it didn't do me any harm'), while others tried to rationalise or understand how situations might have come about, sometimes appearing excessively forgiving of parental shortcomings. Several adopted a resigned or fatalistic approach – 'that's the way it is, there's nothing you can do about it', but a number were openly angry, directing their hostility to either parents, staff or the organisation. However, openly expressed anger seemed to be an emotion people tended to show retrospectively; in childhood there seemed to have been few opportunities to express such negative emotions without incurring repressive consequences. It appeared to be far more common that people had learned to cope with pain by trying to blot out the past, either 'keeping mum' to friends and family about all references to their childhood or, less commonly, by fantasising about the past to some degree, trying to impose an alternative, less negative view on the reality. Indeed, the former approach was strongly advocated by Barnardo's for many years in its advice to its young people: 'Forget about the past and look to the future!' (Bradford, 1994).

Whilst some of these strategies to deal with the pain of the past were more successful than others, all came under severe threat when people took the decision to delve into their past, and were confronted with information which had the effect of triggering a store of buried memories. Many had considered that they were prepared to cope with whatever impact they thought seeing their records would have on them, but most were taken by surprise to some extent at the force of the feelings which the process invoked. Two people in the study made it known that they had sought counselling as a direct result of seeing their records. Ann, who had perhaps the most violent reaction, not so much to reading her records but to seeing the television documentary which preceded this event, rejected counselling. She described however working out her own method of therapy which included writing down all her early memories and feelings to try and 'get them out of her system'.

Even where there was an apparently happy outcome to receiving information such as tracing a birth relative, people were often unprepared for the range and intensity of feelings aroused. The complex issues and emotions surrounding reunions are fairly well-documented in the literature (though most references are to adoption reunions) and have not been extensively addressed in this study. It can be noted however that such literature usually emphasises that:

> Even if it is a successful reunion, it is also a time of emotional stress and adjustment as the past and present come face to face ... the process can raise as many issues as it solves (Children's Society, 1994, p. 15).

The risks of finding or not finding someone, being accepted or rejected, negotiating new relationships, the possibilities of genetic sexual attraction and the effects on other family members are but a few issues which may make the process of reunion an emotional roller-coaster. Tracing, contacting and meeting a birth relative is an experience which usually takes place over a lengthy period. The weeks and months after a reunion may also be a traumatic time, as initial euphoria subsides and sensitive issues from the past come to the surface.

Conclusion

The subjects of this study are exceptional people in many respects. Their varied and often difficult childhood experiences have led them to develop strong feelings about issues which many others take for granted – the meaning of roots, the importance of blood ties, a sense of identity and belonging. Coping with uncertainty and ignorance about their origins has been a significant part of their lives, affecting their relationships with others as well as their feelings about themselves, though its impact has varied for each individual and at different points in their lives. Their experiences of learning about their origins have also been highly unusual. In place of a gradual, lifelong, often unconscious assimilation of knowledge and understanding about their heritage and genealogy, they have, in many cases, acquired much of this information at one point in time. Furthermore the information has been acquired not from sources within their own families, but from 'official' sources, over whose manner and timing of dissemination of information they had little or no control. What has been shown by this study is that an understanding of all these factors which have shaped people's lives is necessary in order to fully appreciate the impact of gaining such information, and to be able to appropriately respond to the needs of people requesting this service.

The combined factors of the intense emotional impact of receiving information about origins, the unpreparedness of many who request information for such an impact, and the length of time following initial receipt of information during which recipients may feel vulnerable and in need of support all have implications for the provision of services to this group of people. This is the final area to be addressed in this study.

11 Implications for Practice

My aim in this study was to seek greater understanding of what it means to learn about one's roots in later life, having grown up apart from one's birth family in the care of an agency. I did not set out to evaluate the services which provide this information, but hope that a greater awareness of the impact of undergoing this unusual experience may have potential benefits both for those seeking such information and those in any way responsible for delivering this service, whether practitioners, managers or policy-makers. From the study has come overriding confirmation of the message that this service is about much more than just the disseminating of information; it cannot be likened to a sort of reference library issuing information to anyone on production of a membership card. On the contrary it entails complex and difficult tasks requiring specialist professional skills and judgements at all levels.

The findings of the study also have implications for current social work policy and practice with separated children, and their needs for knowledge and understanding about their family background and heritage. The study has also highlighted gaps in the existing literature on the subject which would benefit from further research. The people I interviewed are 'extraordinary' people in every sense; but from their experiences much can be learned.

Implications for Current Policy and Practice with Separated Children

This study has confirmed the findings of much recent adoption literature which shows the importance throughout life of information about origins (for example, Haimes and Timms, 1985; Howe and Hinings, 1987; Walby and Symons, 1990; Brodzinsky and Schechter, 1990; Ryburn, 1994). This has been increasingly recognised in child care practice, and was endorsed in legislation in the 1989 Children Act, which seeks to actively promote links with parents, even when the child may not return to live with them. There are also moves to develop more open adoption practice (Ryburn, 1992 and 1994), and recognition that this can be achieved successfully even where there is initial parental opposition (Fratter, 1991). However, recent research evidence

108

(Harrison and Masson, 1994) suggests that social workers have not always translated a belief in the importance of promoting links with parents into practice:

> In many cases parents' legal right of access has been terminated, or access has not been encouraged and has consequently foundered over the course of time (p. 40).

There is therefore a need to emphasise the importance of on-going communication with children about their families and heritage. This is not just a matter of a 'one-off' giving of information, but of enabling continuing open access to appropriate information throughout the child's life. Walby and Symons (1990) stress the importance of providing subsequent opportunities to reiterate and explore the meanings and implications of the information at different stages of the child's development (p. 79) They also acknowledge the stresses and difficulties of putting this into practice. There are practice implications here for the training not only of social workers but also of foster carers and residential staff working with children.

This leads on to implications for practitioners currently compiling records on children being looked after away from home. There are practice implications regarding the format and content of children's records. When adults came to read their records, what they wanted to know was who their birth families were – including putative fathers; their nationality and ethnic origin, state of health, what they looked like, and preferably an indication of their character. Photographs would have been greatly welcomed. It was particularly important to find out why they were placed in care, and what contact their families may have had since separation. It was especially important to those who had had bad or abusive experiences in care to see records of their time in care which might help them make sense of what had happened – how decisions were made and by whom, and what others had thought of them.

Lessons from the past reinforce current growing awareness of the importance of keeping accurate, non-judgemental, nondiscriminatory records. The nature of the agency under whose auspices an individual is brought up may determine the way in which that person's records or history is constructed. Whether a statutory or voluntary agency is involved, admission to 'care' may necessitate making out a case which highlights grounds of sufficient seriousness to merit admission. Thus certain facts and 'truths' are selected to become the 'authorised version' of an individual's history, whilst the accounts of others in that person's life may be omitted, marginalised, distorted or deemed pathological. Cohen (1995) expounds the post-structuralist's view that it is impossible to achieve one 'true' version of a person's story. He highlights the dangers in recording practice of imposing a single 'authorised' storyline on to the densely woven complexities of someone's life history, and advocates the 'open archive' as a means of collecting the diversity of representations which form a person's life story. These, he suggests, can be continually revised or updated, and because there is no narrative structure imposed on it the child – or adult – is free to associate different meanings to it at different times of their life.

The enormous importance attached to their childcare records by those seeking information in later life has significant implications for the *storage and availability of the records*. Policies regarding how long and in what format records are stored appear to vary tremendously between agencies. The childcare records of some interviewees in my study dated back 70 years, and were certainly no less significant to the recipient in later life. Barnardo's receives many requests from relatives wanting information about their late parents or grandparents who were once in Barnardo's care, perhaps to enable them to gain a more complete sense of their own identity and heritage. Such requests raise difficult questions of confidentiality and ownership of personal information, but they also reinforce the importance of preserving information for an appropriate length of time, which may be longer than an individual's lifespan.

It is to be hoped that computerisation of current and future childcare records will facilitate easier and speedier responses to enquiries for access to records. Barnardo's is typical of many voluntary agencies whose records date back to the Victorian era, in that a variety of systems of record-keeping were used over the years, making searches complex and time-consuming. Prior to the second world war, many of Barnardo's records were handwritten in large, heavy ledgers, with entries annotated in different coloured inks or even in pencil. Illegible handwriting, unexplained abbreviations, fading of ink and the deterioration of age and heavy usage combine to complicate and slow down the attempt to compile an individual's records. Fortunately, and remarkably despite the storage of its records at its then headquarters in Stepney throughout the ravages of the second world war, some 372,000 records have survived, dating back to 1867.

The storage of agencies' records today requires no less careful consideration – issues of security, preservation and protection from fire and water damage are all essential (and have resource implications) if future generations are to benefit from access to their personal information.

Implications for Current Policy with Adults Seeking Information

Increasing recognition of the importance of gaining full information about both family background and time in care, together with feedback from service users, led Barnardo's to adopt a policy of 'open access' (or 'direct access') to files. Instead of receiving a file summary, since 1995 people have been able to read their original records in full, subject to 'duty of care' considerations and the deletion of third party information. In my study, Jean strongly endorses this approach when she comments regretfully on the 'sanitised' version of her life which has been selected (prior to the introduction of open access policies) for her to read, when she would have preferred to 'rifle through' everything which was ever written about her. Although there is no legal obligation on the part of voluntary agencies to make their records available, and their records were never intended for this purpose, the findings of this study confirm the importance of an open access policy. It represents a shift from the 'secrecy' assumptions of the past towards an assumption of openness, and a willingness to consider not whether, but how to enable service users to gain access to records, and how to ensure that they gain maximum benefit from that process.

Despite resource limitations and the existence, in Barnardo's After Care, of an already long waiting list for information, consideration must be given to continuing efforts to make the availability of this service known to other potential users. Past experience has clearly shown that many people had been trying to gain access to their information for a very long time and this study showed that awareness that the records were now accessible was the main trigger for many people's requests for information.

The Needs of Former Child Migrants

The particular needs of former child migrants (from all agencies) for help in coming to terms with their childhood experiences and for information about their past was recently highlighted in a Select Committee report (1998). Its recommendations included setting up a central database, managed and coordinated jointly by the governments involved in child migration, to direct former child migrants or their descendants to more detailed sources of information. It recommended that former child migrants or their descendants should have immediate access to all files containing information concerning their history and background, together with access to therapy and counselling where required. It also proposed setting up a travel fund to enable former child migrants to visit the country of their birth and attend family reunions.

Implications for Current Practice with Adults Seeking Information

It became apparent from both my own and others' studies that people had many different reasons for seeking information, and widely differing expectations of what they would learn. The social worker sharing the records needs to establish what people are seeking without making prior assumptions. Furthermore, apparently similar material may have a very different impact on different people, depending on not only their expectations but particularly on their past experiences, which have shaped their attitudes towards their birth families, the agency, and the importance attached to the blood tie. People's reminiscences have an important role in helping the social worker to understand where the client is coming from.

Social workers working with adults seeking retrospective access to their records have a responsibility to help clients interpret what they read by explaining the historical, social and cultural perspectives in which the records were written. People may be seeking 'truths' and certainties, but need to be aware that what they see is but a version of their origins which was constructed at a particular time and by a particular person for a particular purpose.

It is difficult to underestimate the emotional impact of reading their records for most people. It seemed that few of my interviewees were prepared for the strength of their emotional response to their information, and this is also true of many of the people seen by social workers in Barnardo's After Care. One such example was Brian, a former senior social work practitioner. With more than 30 years of social work behind him, Brian had no concerns about how viewing his records would affect him:

> I was so self-assured, I thought I'd find it a piece of cake. I was going to cope ... but I didn't.

In this case, the information was not even new to Brian – it confirmed for him everything he had thought or guessed about his background, including his mother's part in getting him admitted to Barnardo's. But seeing it in black and white had stunned him:

> It's something I'd lived with forever but reading information that confirms your

experience is another matter. I could not have dealt with papers like that through the post … Reading my records was devastating. It sounds over the top, but it felt as though the social worker who showed me the records saved my life.

Brian had very bad memories of his time in care, and felt he had been deprived of a proper childhood. He admitted,

> You carry such baggage with you for years and years. You need someone who knows about Barnardo's and who has the professional experience to help you pick up the pieces. You need to be able to offload immediately. Fortunately I feel I've had a superb professional service and now I've laid the ghost of my past (*Guild Messenger*, Summer 1998).

Similar feelings were reported by 48 year old Bobbie when she prepared to view her records:

> When they talked about seeing a social worker, I thought what do I need somebody like that for? I can handle all this. I saw my records in three parts. The first time I felt all right. My husband came with me. But the next day I started taking it all in. I just felt very sad, but did not want to let anybody know.
> The second time I saw my records I was on my own. I've never forgotten the journey back. It took me an hour and a half on the train. I could not look at anybody. I had no newspaper to hide behind. That night I had to go to a football match but there was no way I could concentrate on the game. All I wanted to do was to keep reading my notes – over and over again (*Guild Messenger*, Winter 1998).

Pieces of information often acted as triggers to other memories which may have been long buried. Some of these were happy memories but others – such as Ann's memories of abuse by her carers – were distressing and difficult to cope with. The reliving of past feelings arising from separation and loss during the interview with the social worker was a common experience. Social workers in the After Care service find that many people they see suffer very low self-esteem because of their past experiences and this sometimes causes mental health problems. These factors have implications for the support required to deal with the consequences of acquiring such information. It validates the importance attached by Barnardo's After Care team of making a 'duty of care' assessment in each case, which takes into account the person's available support network, state of health and resilience, together with the nature of the information to be shared. In very exceptional circumstances some or all of a person's records may be withheld from them, where an assessment is made that there is risk of serious harm either to the person concerned, their relatives, or to past or present employees of Barnardo's. If this happens, the reasons are explained and a written summary of information will be provided instead. An appeal system is also available.

In order to make such an assessment of the potential impact of seeing one's records, and to provide the appropriate support when required for this very emotional experience, it is considered vital that records are shared in person, rather than through the post. This is a policy which has sometimes been questioned in Barnardo's both by those on After Care's lengthy waiting list and by those responsible for ensuring that limited resources of staffing and budgets are used efficiently and economically. However, the experiences of those who have seen their records have almost without exception confirmed the findings of the study in demonstrating the need for a personal service. Two people who were interviewed in After Care's magazine for those formerly in its care commented upon this policy. The first was a 71 year old who was unable to travel to Barkingside to see his records because of ill-health, and suggested that his records were posted to him. The social worker advised against this and travelled to see him at his home instead. He described his feelings afterwards:

> The information the social worker gave me came as a complete bombshell. It was a new story on the whole of my life. If I'd received it through the post it would have been terrible. I now appreciate having an individual interview. Talking to someone personally allowed me to get over the shock. All my questions were answered very sensitively.

After Care social workers see many people in their 70s and 80s, and this generation have often received the least information about their family background during their childhood in care. Consequently the impact of receiving such information for the first time later in life may be even more powerful than for others. The second comment on the experience came from 78 year old Reg, who came into care aged four, and had had no idea of his background or who his parents were. When he learned of his family's circumstances he wept.

> It made me realise what my mother went through, trying to keep a family of 11 together on her own. Even now when I read through the papers I get tears in my eyes. I thought they would just send a letter through the post, but I'm so glad they didn't. It was very emotional. The social worker I saw was marvellous and explained all the whys and wherefores in so much detail. It was very comforting (*Guild Messenger*, Summer 1998).

Both my own study and other research (Haimes and Timms, 1985; Walby and Symons, 1990; Shekleton, 1990) confirmed that it was common for adults of all backgrounds to find it difficult to ask for information. They expressed fears to researchers of being regarded as abnormal, obsessed or self-indulgent, or seeking something to which they might be denied access. For many people, their meeting with a social worker may have been their first chance to discuss their early childhood experiences. Concerns about what will be uncovered in their records and what memories may arise meant that people were often anxious and nervous during the visit. These anxieties sometimes made it difficult to absorb what was actually being said or seen in the interview with the social worker. All these factors highlight the usefulness of providing written material prior to the interview to prepare the client for the nature and impact of the information, and also the value of offering a follow up afterwards when the person has had an opportunity to reflect on what they have learned.

The historical neglect of a black perspective in most records makes it all the more vital that this area is acknowledged and addressed when information is shared. Having access to a black worker may be very helpful in allowing issues of racism both in the records and in childcare experiences to be raised. Shekleton's research (1990) showed how black and mixed race adults were especially wary about approaching agencies to seek information about their origins for fear of being seen as dysfunctional.

After Care social workers are only too aware that some people need considerably more support, counselling or therapy than can be provided in a brief intervention. Barnardo's are not alone in having to offer services within severe resource constraints, which greatly restrict the extent to which long term support can be provided. Training in 'brief therapy' techniques has been one creative and constructive approach to addressing this issue, but does not eliminate the need for strategies to enable those who want it to receive further counselling, therapy or support. Specialist help in this area is difficult to access, particularly for those without the financial resources to pay for private counselling, and whose needs do not fall within the remit of statutory mental health agencies. There is at present no comparable independent agency to the Post-Adoption Centre for those who grew up in care. There is however considerable scope for further development of services to those who need help in coming to terms with their past or in tracing family members from whom they became separated, or who would welcome support through the emotional ups and downs of newly-developing relationships to be negotiated following reunions. After Care social workers give advice on tracing and may undertake tracing work themselves where the person requesting help is very elderly or vulnerable or where other agencies are unable to help. However this work is very time-consuming and has to be limited by pressure of resources and the demands of a long waiting list.

Whatever the method of tracing used, social workers play an important role in preparing people for reunions with relatives, to ensure that they have thought through the possible issues involved and considered the possible outcomes. The offer of support throughout the reunion process is always made, but some may not take up the offer, whilst others may seek longer-term support than it is possible to offer, again within the restraints of limited resources.

The complexities and the emotional intensity of the issues around information sharing, as well as the related areas of tracing relatives and preparing for reunions, highlight the need for social workers to have appropriate skills and training, especially awareness of issues of loss, identity, and attachment. Difficult judgements have to be made about the likely impact of sharing information which may shock or distress – for example imparting details of an incestuous birth, or serious parental neglect or cruelty. The language used to describe both parents and children in records is often harsh and judgemental, and childcare reports may be overwhelmingly negative in tone and detail. Many people who come to read their records are already vulnerable and lacking in self-esteem. The emotional impact upon the worker of constantly sharing such powerful and often difficult information, and the unpredictable response that it invokes, cannot be underestimated. The phenomenon of 'secondary trauma' is just beginning to be recognised as a significant reality in this type of work. This has implications for the supervision and support of workers in this area if they are to sustain a sensitive and skilled response to those seeking to make sense of their past. It is hoped that a greater understanding of the meaning and impact of sharing and receiving information will serve to reinforce the importance of maintaining and resourcing a high quality service to meet the needs of those who need it.

APPENDICES

1   Research Outline

1.   Research Topic

The impact of receiving family background information upon adults who grew up in Barnardo's care.

2.   Researcher

I am a part-time research student at the University of East Anglia undertaking a Masters degree in the School of Social Work. My qualifications are:

> BA (Hons) Social Administration (1974);
> CQSW (1976);
> Advanced Certificate in Social Work (1995).

I am employed by Barnardo's as a social worker in the After Care Section, and have previous experience in local authority family placement work.

3.   Funding

The research is being carried out in my own time under the auspices of UEA and is funded independently. The research will only be carried out with the full knowledge and consent of Barnardo's in order to obtain access to potential participants, but I accept full responsibility for the initiation, design and outcome of the study.

4.   Methodology

This will be a small qualitative research study. It is aimed to complete 12-15 interviews. A sample will be selected from Barnardo's After Care records of those who have received family background information from that agency at least 12 months previously. By reference to files and by discussion with After care staff it is aimed to identify:

a) potentially 'information rich' cases (i.e. good interview subjects);

b) a diversity of ages and backgrounds;

c) those located accessibly geographically for interviewing.

Those receiving on-going counselling and those with severe psychiatric disorders will not be approached.

Potential respondents will be approached by letter (attached) from myself. Participation in a taped interview will be invited to explore their experiences and feelings about the impact of acquiring information about their family background.

Those willing to be interviewed will be fully informed about the confidential and voluntary nature of their participation and will be asked to sign a form of consent.

5.   Confidentiality

All interview material will be strictly confidential and access will only be by myself under the supervision of UEA. Material from interviews may be quoted in the research report but participants' names will not be used and care will be taken to ensure that no material will be linked in an identifiable way to individuals. All research notes and tape recordings will be destroyed after publication.

6.   Use of Research Material

The information gathered will form part of a thesis to be submitted for a Masters degree. It may also be published in appropriate formats in other outlets, with the aim of disseminating as widely as possible findings which may be of help both to those seeking to make sense of their own past and to those responsible for offering services to people seeking family background information. It is hoped that any increase in understanding of the impact upon those who trace their origins will lead, directly or indirectly to an improvement in the quality of services offered to them.

2   Interview Guide

1. Motivation

What led you to ask Barnardo's for your information?
(Including why then?)
Did you discuss your plans with anyone beforehand?

2. Aims and expectations

What were you hoping to get from your search? What did you expect to happen/
find?

3. Prior knowledge

How much information did you already know about your past? How did you
find out?

4. Childhood experiences

How would you describe your childhood?
– prior to admission to care?
– in care?
Age at admission?
Did you wonder about your origins as a child? Any fantasies? At what stage?
Feelings about Barnardo's?

5. Feelings about the process of receiving information

Can you recall the occasion on which you read your records – time, place,
social worker, etc? What did you learn? What were your feelings at the time?
Do you have any thoughts/comments about the way the information was shared
with you?

6. Outcome of receiving information

- Have you found out any more information since your last contact with Barnardo's After Care? Where from? Nature of information ?
- Have you traced, or tried to trace, any relatives? Outcome?
- Before you knew about your past, how did you feel about yourself? How did you feel about being in care? Do you feel any differently now?
- Since receiving your information, have there been any changes in:

  • your relationships with anyone close to you (e.g. partner, children, parents, former carers)?
  • your employment or interests?
  • your health (physical or mental)? Do you feel more 'at peace'/ unsettled?
  • any other areas of your life?

If so, do you link any of these with learning more about your past? In what way?

7. Any other comments

Would there be any advice you'd give to someone else thinking of seeking information about their past?

Bibliography

Adams, G. and Shea, J. (1979), 'The relationship between identity status, locus of control, and ego development', *Journal of Youth and Adolescence*, 8.

Aldgate, J. (1988), 'Work with children experiencing separation and loss' in Aldgate, J. and Simmonds, J. (eds), *Direct Work with Children*, BAAF, Batsford.

Aumend, S. and Barrett, M. (1984), 'Self-concept and attitudes toward adoption: a comparison of searching and non-searching adult adoptees', *Child Welfare*, 63, pp. 251–9.

Bagley, C. and Young, L. (1979), 'The identity, adjustment and achievement of transracially adopted children' in Verma, G. and Bagley, C. (eds), *Race, Education and Identity*, London, Macmillan, pp. 192–219.

Begley, V.J. (1988), *Missing Links*, Chevy Chase, USA.

Berridge, D. (1997), *Foster Care: A research review*, The Stationery Office, London.

Berridge, D. and Brodie, I. (1996), 'Residential care in England and Wales: the Inquiries and after' in Hill, M. and Aldgate, J. (1996), *Child Welfare Services*, Jessica Kingsley Publishers, London and USA (chapter 13).

Berridge, D. and Cleaver, H. (1987), *Foster Home Breakdown*, Basil Blackwell, Oxford and London.

Bowlby, J. (1951), *Maternal Care and Mental Health*, World Health Organisation (WHO), Geneva.

Bowlby, J. (1969), *Attachment and Loss: Vol. 1. Attachment*, Hogarth Press, London.

Bowlby, J. (1973), *Attachment and Loss: Vol. 2. Separation, Anxiety and Anger*, Hogarth Press, London.

Bradford, C. (1994), Revealing Histories Barnardo's (unpublished).

Bradford, C. (1998), 'Starved of facts', *Barnardo's Guild Messenger*, 315, p. 28.

Brodzinsky, D. (1987), 'Adjustment to adoption: a psychosocial perspective', *Clinical Psychology Review*, 7, pp. 25–47.

Brodzinsky, D. (1990), 'Surrendering an infant for adoption: the birthmother experience' in Brodzinsky, D. and Schechter, M. (eds) (1990), *Psychology of Adoption*, Oxford University Press, Oxford.

Brodzinsky, D. and Schechter, M. (eds) (1990), *Psychology of Adoption*, Oxford University Press, Oxford.

Brodzinsky, D., Schechter, M. and Henig, R. (1992), *Being Adopted: The lifelong search for self*, Doubleday, New York.

Bullock, R. (1993), *Residential Care of Children: A review of the research*, Department of Health, London.

Cheetham, J. (1972), *Social Work with Immigrants*, Routledge and Kegan Paul, London.

Child Adoption Committee (1925), *First Report* (Cmnd. 2401), HMSO (Tomlin Report).

Children's Society (1994), *Preparing for Reunion*, Children's Society, London.

Clarke, A. and Clarke, A. (1976), *Early Experience: Myth and evidence*, Free Press New York.

Clothie, F. (1943), 'The psychology of the adopted child', *Mental Hygiene*, 27, pp. 222–30.

Cohen, P. (1995), *Frameworks for a Study of Adoptive Identities*, Centre for Adoption and Identity Studies, University of East London.

Copeman, T. (1989), *Mother's Son*, Maclean Dubois.

Day, C. (1979), 'Access to birth records: General Register Office study', *Adoption and Fostering*, 98, 4, pp. 17–28.

Department of Health (1995), *Looking After Children*, HMSO, London.

Derrida, J. (1978), *Writing and Difference*, University of Chicago Press, Chicago.

Dummett, A. (1973), *Portrait of Racism in the United Kingdom*, Penguin, Harmondsworth.

Erikson, E. (1959), 'Identity and the life cycle', *Psychological Issues*, Vol. 1, p. 1.

Erikson, E. (1963), *Childhood and Society*, Penguin, Harmondsworth.

Erikson, E. (1968), *Identity: Youth and Crisis*, Faber and Faber, London.

Erikson, E. (1980), *Identity and the Life Cycle*, Norton, New York.

Fahlberg, V. (1981), *Attachment and Separation*, BAAF, Batsford.

Feast, J. (1992), 'Working in the adoption circle – outcomes of Section 51 counselling', *Adoption and Fostering*, 16, 4, pp. 46–52.

Feast, J. and Howe, D. (1997), 'Adopted adults who search for background information and contact with birth relatives', *Adoption and Fostering*, 21, 2, pp. 8–15.

Fletcher, B. (1993), *Not Just a Name – The views of young people in foster and residential care*, National Consumer Council/Who Cares? Trust, London.

Fonagy, P., Steele, M., Steele, H., Higgit, A. and Target, M. (1994), 'The theory and practice of resilience', *Journal of Child Psychology and Psychiatry*, 35, 2, pp. 231–57.

Fox Harding, L. (1991), *Perspectives in Child Care Policy*, Longman, London and New York.

Fratter, J. (1991), 'Adoptive parents and open adoption in the UK' in Mullender, A. (ed.), *Open Adoption*, BAAF, Batsford.

Fratter, J. (1994), 'Perspectives on adoption with contact: implications for policy and practice', doctoral thesis, Cranfield University.

Freeman, I., Morrison, A., Lockhart, F. and Swanson, M. (1996), 'Consulting service users : the views of young people' in Hill, M. and Aldgate, J. (eds), *Child Welfare Services: Developments in law, policy, practice and research*, Jessica Kingsley Publishers London and New York (chapter 16).

George, V. (1970), *Foster Care: Theory and practice*, Routledge and Kegan Paul, London.

Gill, O. and Jackson, B. (1983), *Adoption and Race: Black, Asian and mixed race children in white families*, BAAF, Batsford.

Gilligan, C. (1982), *In a Different Voice: Psychological theory and women's development*, Harvard University Press, Cambridge, MA.

Glaser, B. and Strauss, A. (1967), *The Discovery of Grounded Theory*, Aldine, Chicago.

Goffman, E. (1963), *Stigma: Notes on the management of spoiled identity*, Penguin, Harmondsworth.

Goldstein, J., Freud, A. and Solnit, A. (1973), *Beyond the Best Interests of the Child*, Free Press, New York.

Goldstein, J., Freud, A. and Solnit, A. (1979), *Before the Best Interests of the Child*, Free Press, New York.

Haimes, E. and Timms, N. (1985), *Adoption, Identity and Social Policy: The search for distant relatives*, Gower, Aldershot.

Harrison, C. and Masson, J. (1994), 'Working in partnership with "lost" parents', *Adoption and Fostering*, 18, 1, pp. 40–4.

Hill, M., Lambert, L. and Trisiliotis, J. (1989), *Achieving Adoption with Love and Money*, National Children's Bureau, London.

Hodgkins, P. (1987), *Adopted Adults: An evaluation of their relationships with their families*, NORCAP Publications, Oxford.

Hodgkins, P. (1991), *Birth Records Counselling – a practical guide*, BAAF, Batsford.

Holman, R. (1980), 'Exclusive and inclusive concepts of fostering' in Triseliotis, J. (ed.), *New Developments in Foster Care and Adoption*, Routledge and Kegan Paul, London (chapter 5).

Howard, S. and Kubis, J. (1964), 'Ego identity and some aspects of personal functioning', *Journal of Psychology*, 58.

Howe, D. (1995), *Attachment Theory for Social Work Practice*, Macmillan, London.

Howe, D. (1996), 'Adopters' relationships with their adopted children from adolescence to early adulthood', *Adoption and Fostering*, 20, 3, pp. 35–44.

Howe, D. (1997), *Patterns of Adoption: Nature, nurture and psychosocial development*, Blackwell Science, Oxford.

Howe, D. and Hinings, D. (1987), 'Adopted children referred to a child and family centre', *Adoption and Fostering*, 11, 3, p. 44.

Humphreys, M. (1994), *Empty Cradles*, Doubleday, New York.

Husband, C. (1986), 'Racism, prejudice and social policy' in Combe, V. and Little, A. (eds), *Race and Social Work*, Tavistock Press, London.

Jewett, C. (1984), *Helping Children Cope with Separation and Loss*, BAAF, Batsford.

Kahan, B. (1979), *Growing Up in Care*, Blackwell, Oxford.

Klein, M. (1948), *Contributions to Psycho-analysis, 1921–1945*, Hogarth Press, London.

Klein, M. (1959), *Our Adult World and its Roots in Infancy*, Tavistock Press, London.

Kornitzer, M. (1971), 'The adopted adolescent and the sense of identity', *Child Adoption*, 66, pp. 43–8.

Kubler-Ross, E. (1972), *Death and Dying*, Tavistock Press, London.

Leeding, A. (1977), 'Access to birth records', *Adoption and Fostering*, 1, 3, pp. 19–25.

Lifton, B. (1988), *Lost and Found – the adoption experience*, Harper and Row, New York.

Lindsay, M. and McGarry, K. (1984), *Adoption Counselling – A talking point*, Barnardo's Scottish Division.

Lofland, J. and Lofland, L. (1984), *Analysing Social Settings: A guide to qualitative observation and analysis*, 2nd edn, Wadsworth, Belmont, CA.

Marcia, J. (1967), 'Ego identity status: relationship to change in self-esteem, "General Maladjustment" and "'Authoritarianism'", *Journal of Personality*, 35.

Marcia, J. (1980), 'Identity in adolescence' in Adelson, J. (ed.), *Handbook of Adolescent Psychology*, Wiley, New York.

McWhinnie, A. (1967), *Adopted Children: How they grew up*, Routledge and Kegan Paul, London.

McWhinnie, A. (1994), 'The concept of "open adoption" – how valid is it?' on McWhinnie, A. and Smith, J. (eds), *Current Human Dilemmas in Adoption*, University of Dundee, Dundee, pp. 7–32.

Millham, S., Bullock, R., Hosie, K. and Haak, M. (1986), *Lost in Care: Problems of maintaining links between children in care and their families*, Gower, Aldershot.

Office of Population Censuses and Surveys (1992), *Series DH1. Mortality statistics: surveillance (Time trends)*, HMSO, London.

Page, R. and Clark, G. (1977), *Who Cares? Young People Speak Out*, National Childrens Bureau, London.

Parish, A. and Cotton, P. (1988), *Original Thoughts: The views of adult adoptees and birth families following renewed contact*, Barnardo's, London.

Parker, R. (1966), *Decisions in Child Care*, George Allen and Unwin, London.

Parker, R. (1990), *Away from Home: A history of child care*, Barnardo's, London.

Patton, M. (1990), *Qualitative Evaluation and Research Methods*, 2nd edn, Sage, Newbury Park.

Pringle, M.K. (1980), *The Needs of Children*, Hutchinson, London.

Pugh, G. (ed.) (1993), *30 Years of Change for Children*, National Children's Bureau, London.

Read, D., Adams, G. and Dobson, W. (1984), ,Ego-identity, personality and social influence style', *Journal of Personality and Social Psychology*, 46.

Robson, C. (1993), *Real World Research*, Blackwell, Oxford and Cambridge, MA.

Rowe, J. and Lambert, L. (1973), *Children Who Wait*, Association of British Adoption Agencies.

Rowe, J., Hundleby, M. and Garnett, L. (1989), *Child Care Now: A survey of placement patterns*, BAAF, Batsford.

Rutter, M. (1981), 'Stress, coping and development', *Journal of Child Psychology and Psychiatry*, 22, p. 4.

Rutter, M. (1985), 'Resilience in the face of adversity', *British Journal of Psychiatry*, 147.

Rutter, M., Quinton, D. and Liddle, C. (1983), 'Parenting in two generations' in Madge, N. (ed.), *Families at Risk*, DHSS, London.

Ryburn, M. (1992), *Adoption in the 1990s: Identity and openness*, Leamington Press,

Ryburn, M. (1994), *Open Adoption: Research,Theory, and Practice*, Gower, Aldershot.

Ryburn, M. (1995), 'Secrecy and openess in adoption: an historical perspective', *Social Policy and Administration*, 29, 2, pp. 150–68.

Sachdeve, P. (1992), 'Adoption reunion and after: a study of the search process and experience of adoptees', *Child Welfare*, 71, 1, pp. 53–68.

Sanders, P. and Sitterly, N. (1981), *Search Aftermath and Adjustments*, NSW Committee on Adoption, Australia.

Sandler, J. (1961), 'Identification in children, parents and doctors' in MacKeith, R. and Sandler, J. (eds), *Psychosomatic Aspects of Paediatrics*, Pergamon, Oxford.

Sants, H. (1965), 'Genealogical bewilderment in children with substitute parents', *Child Adoption*, 47, pp. 32–42.

Sawbridge, P. (1988), 'The Post-Adoption Centre – what are the users teaching us?', *Adoption and Fostering*, 12, 1, pp. 5–12.

Sawbridge, P. (1990), 'Post-Adoption Counselling: what do we actually do?', *Adoption and Fostering*, 14, 1, pp. 31–4.

Schaffer, H. (1990), *Making Decisions about Children: Psychological questions and answers*, Blackwell, Oxford.

Shekleton, J. (1990), *A Glimpse Through the Looking Glass: Post-Adoption Centre Discussion Paper no. 8*, Post-Adoption Centre, London.

Shweder, R. and Bourne, E. (1982), 'Does the concept of the person vary cross-culturally?' in Marsella, A. and White, G. (eds), *Cultural Concepts of Mental Health and Therapy*, Reidal, Boston.

Simon, R. and Altstein, H. (1977), *Transracial Adoption*, Wiley Interscience, New York.

Simon, R. and Altstein, H. (1981), *Transracial Adoption: a follow-up*, Lexington Books, New York.

Small, J. (1986), 'Transracial placements: conflicts and contradictions' in Ahmed, S., Cheetham, J. and Small, J. (eds), *Social Work with Black Children and their Families*, BAAF, Batsford.

Stark, P. and Traxler, F. (1974), 'Empirical validation of Erikson's theory of identity crises in late adolescence', *Journal of Psychology*, 86.

Strauss, A. and Corbin, J. (1990), *Basics of Qualitative Research: Grounded theory procedures and techniques*, Sage, Newbury Park.

Sugarman, L. (1986), *Lifespan Development*, Methuen, London and New York.

Thoburn, J. (1988), *Child Placement: Principles and practice*, London, Widwood House.

Tizard, B. and Phoenix, A. (1994), 'Black identity and transracial adoption' in Gaber, I. and Aldridge, J. (eds), *In the Best Interests of the Child*, Free Association Books, London.

Trasler, G. (1960), *In Place of Parents*, Routledge and Kegan Paul, London.

Trinder, L. (1996), 'Social work research: the state of the art (or science)', *Child and Family Social Work*, 1, pp. 233–42.

Triseliotis, J. (1973), *In Search of Origins: The experiences of adopted people*, Routledge and Kegan Paul, London.

Triseliotis, J. (1980), *New Developments in Foster Care and Adoption*, Routledge and Kegan Paul, London.

Triseliotis, J. (1984), 'Obtaining birth certificates' in Bean, P. (ed.), *Adoption: Essays in social policy, law and sociology*, Tavistock Press, London.

Triseliotis, J., Borland, M., Hill, M. and Lambert, L. (1995), *Teenagers and the Social Work Services*, HMSO, London.

Triseliotis, J. and Hill, M. (1990), 'Contrasting adoption, foster care, and residential rearing' in Brodzinsky, D. and Schechter, M. (1990), The Psychology of Adoption, Oxford University Press, Oxford.

Triseliotis, J. and Russell, J. (1984), *Hard to Place: The outcome of adoption and residential care*, Heinemann, London.

Walby, C. and Symons, B. (1990), *Who am I? Identity, adoption and human fertilisation*, Batsford, BAAF.

Ward, H. (ed.) (1995), *Looking After Children: Research into Practice*, HMSO, London.